GROWING OLDER

OTHER BOOKS BY JOHN LANGONE

BOMBED, BUZZED, SMASHED OR . . . SOBER
A Book about Alcohol

DEAD END
A Book about Suicide

DEATH IS A NOUN
A View of the End of Life

GOODBYE TO BEDLAM
Understanding Mental Illness and Retardation

HUMAN ENGINEERING
Marvel or Menace?

LIFE AT THE BOTTOM
The People of Antarctica

LIKE, LOVE, LUST
A View of Sex and Sexuality

LONG LIFE
What We Know and Are Learning about the Aging Process

THORNY ISSUES
How Ethics and Morality Affect the Way We Live

VIOLENCE!
Our Fastest-Growing Public Health Problem

VITAL SIGNS
The Way We Die in America

GROWING OLDER

What Young People Should Know about Aging

JOHN LANGONE

Little, Brown and Company
Boston   Toronto   London

For my uncle, Mayo C.

First Edition

Library of Congress Cataloging-in-Publication Data

Langone, John, 1929–
    Growing older: what young people should know about aging / by John Langone. — 1st ed.
        p.   cm.
    Includes index.
    Summary: Discusses some of the truths, myths, and popular misconceptions of the aging process.
    ISBN 0-316-51459-4
    1. Aged — United States — Juvenile literature.   2. Aging — United States — Juvenile literature.   [1. Aged.   2. Aging.   3. Old Age.]
I. Title.
HQ1064.U5L335   1991
305.26′0973 — dc20   90-38434

10 9 8 7 6 5 4 3 2 1

HC

Published simultaneously in Canada
by Little, Brown & Company (Canada) Limited

Printed in the United States of America

CONTENTS

1 ∎ WHY SHOULD A TEENAGER KNOW ABOUT BEING OLD?

"The future has a habit of suddenly and dramatically becoming the present."
— Roger Babson

Growing old — what does it mean? When you were in first grade, sixth-graders were "the big kids." People in high school were practically adults. Your parents were decidedly "old" and your grandparents were "aged." Growing up was something you expected, but aging, growing old, would never happen to you.

Biologically speaking, aging is a process that begins from the moment we are conceived in our mothers' wombs. You are aging right now, just as I am, writing these words at age fifty-nine. And what of "old"? You probably think of me as old; my mother, who is eighty-three, thinks of me as young. The people who are wished a happy hundredth (or more) birthday each morning by Willard Scott on the *Today* show think of me as a mere child.

Old, then, seems to be a relative term. Anyone who wonders what it means should be asked, compared with whom? Or with what? No one is born *old*, but we are all *aging* as part of the slow process that begins at conception and keeps on heading us steadily toward our allotted biblical threescore and ten. Perhaps there will be a bit more tacked on — if we are lucky, if we have the right genetic blueprints that gave us long-lived ancestors, if we follow the right diet, live in the right environment, have the right job and mental attitude. If we are very lucky and don't have a serious accident or a premature illness, we may make it to "a hundred and change," as the car salespeople put it.

In preparing this book, I asked two teachers, Alice Yacobian and Chuck Ozug of Hingham High School in Massachusetts, to ask a group of teenagers to answer three questions, these two among them: How old is old? How are old people different? The answers may or may not surprise you. I suggest that you read them carefully and ask yourself which comments you agree or disagree with.

"Old is probably over eighty. Old people are different because of their age, appearance, thinking, and sometimes health."

"I think thirty is old. Well, old people can't see very good and are not active."

"Sixty is old, and old people are different because they become lazy."

"Old is about forty. Their skin gets all wrinkled, and they become grumpy."

"Almost any age as long as you have gray hair. They're supposed to be different and wiser, but sometimes I don't think they're too swift."

"Ninety-six. They're different from me in that their clothes are out of style and they tell stories about when they were my age way back when."

"Old is when people start to feel superior to people under thirty and when they don't get proper respect. Different? Yes. They listen to Mel Tormé and Robert Goulet when we listen to U2 and Guns 'n' Roses."

"Old is the age that you realize climbing stairs is more difficult than cooking a seven-course meal. Old people are different because they have more memories."

"I think old is my parents' ages and older. They are different because they are the most caring people, like my grandparents."

"You are old when you can no longer act young. Different because they may not agree with my ideas about clothes or music."

"Old is a lifestyle. You never have to be old unless you want to be. Old people are wiser, but weaker than us."

"I think old is really an undefinable number to establish. Old could mean old as in, like, your grandparents, or old when people are always sick. I also think of my parents as old. They don't seem to enjoy life as easy as myself and other kids my age. Old people are different from me in that they are more boring. They seem to be interested in trivial things that don't interest me."

"Old age is not determined by physical appearance or the number of years one has lived, but by the loss of ability to enjoy life and to live with adventure. It is unfortunate how many people forget how to appreciate people and events for what they are, and instead dwell on the evil and inconvenience of the world. The elderly are bitter complainers. Old people lack my youthful outlook on life, that of opportunity and promise for the future."

"Old, to me, seems anybody that has stopped living life to the fullest, anybody who doesn't love and have fun with life anymore. It isn't really possible to put an age on 'old' as there are teenagers who seem old, yet there are senior citizens who seem young."

"Old is a state of mind. You could be old at twenty or young at seventy-five. It all depends on how you live, how you treat yourself, how you treat others, how much confidence you have (or don't have) and just who you are. Old people aren't different because of how they look or walk, but because of how they lived their lives."

"You can't measure old by an age. I've had kids call me old — and I'm only fifteen. What's different about old people is that they can teach us a lot about wars, people, and dates of historical stuff. People seem to see them as a burden, but we can learn from them."

"I guess seventy-five is old. Most old people I know seem happier. I'm kind of jealous of them because they've made it through life, and I'm afraid I won't."

"Old is when people go to nursing homes. They are all-knowing, but can't express it because they can't remember. But, then, teenagers think they know everything and say so, but they don't, really."

"Old is when you let your age affect your personality and you get crabby. They're usually a pain in the ass."

As you read on, it might not be a bad idea to come back to these replies. You may then want to ask yourself: which ones make more sense now? Why did some of the students answer the way they did? Which of them really know and understand old people?

Many of these replies will be dealt with, in one way or other, in this book. After you finish it, you may know more about aging than you ever wanted to. But this might be more important than you realize because while you are generally being trained and educated to look to the future — how to choose a career, improve your physical and mental health, live longer, and become a good parent — learning about the aging process and how to plan for it has not usually been part of that education. The noted behavioral psychologist B. F. Skinner has underscored the necessity of your knowing more about aging. "A good time to think about old age," he said, "is when you are young, because you can then do much to improve the chances that you will enjoy it when it comes. . . . Old age is rather like another country. You will enjoy it more if you have prepared yourself before you go."[1]

Good advice. Perhaps people who have not aged too well — those who, like some of the elderly pictured in the students' replies, are crabby or intolerant — might be a bit happier if they had anticipated old age, readied themselves for it. People who do not prepare for old age are also at risk of forming the wrong ideas about what it means to age and become old. They may believe, for instance, that all older people have to live in nursing homes, or that they lose their memories, their wit, and their intelligence. People who lack information about the aging process may be all too quick to jump to the erroneous conclusions that the elderly lose their need to be attractive to the opposite sex, that everyone over sixty should retire, that old folks cannot play any game more strenuous than bingo or checkers, that they all need medicine to survive, that they prefer to hang out only with other old people, that they do not belong behind a desk in school, that they can never have any more peak experiences. We will try to provide as much information about aging as possible and, by so doing, attempt to dispel some of those misconceptions and myths about the elderly.

A familiar expression, "You are never too old to learn," is generally taken to mean that no matter how much experience and wisdom a person has, there is always something new that he or she does not know. We can turn that expression around to say, "You're never too young to learn about aging." While you may feel you cannot especially relate to aging and old age — somewhat like the farm kid who is not interested in learning about city life because it's not his or her way of life — it is imperative that you try. In the not-too-distant future, you will become your parents and grandparents. You can count on it, more than you can count on anything else in this world. As Groucho Marx once observed, "It's easy to grow old. All you have to do is live long enough."

2 ■
WHO ARE THE ELDERLY?

"To me, old age is fifteen years older than I am."
— Bernard Baruch

Americans and people in the rest of the world are growing older. It you doubt it, just look around. Twelve out of every hundred people in our country today are over sixty-five, the number that is the standard milestone for "old age." In the next year or so, there will be more men and women here over that age than the total number of Americans alive during the Civil War. By the year 2020, twenty out of a hundred will be over sixty-five. Five years after that, according to the Population Reference Bureau, the elderly will outnumber teenagers by two to one. Contrast that with fifty years ago when only four out of a hundred people were sixty-five or over.

The United States is not alone in the graying of its population. Sweden, with 17 percent of its people over sixty-five, has the oldest population in the world. Other countries, like Japan, are catching up: Japan's elderly population has tripled since the end of World War II and now stands at around 11 million.

Because of better nutrition, improved living conditions, and advances in medical science, not only are there more elderly, but they are living longer than they ever did. During Julius Caesar's reign, the average life span of a Roman was twenty-five years. A child born around the time of the American Revolution, in 1776, could expect to live to about thirty-five; for a child born in 1900, it was forty-seven. Those dismal numbers have changed dramatically. A child born in the United States today has about seventy-five years of life to look forward to; a man of sixty-five can expect to live almost to age seventy-nine, a woman to eighty-three. (Women generally outlive men because of biological and environmental factors we will look at later.) Indeed, in the twenty-five years from 1953 to 1978, the number of Americans over the age of eighty-five has tripled: from 700,000 to 2.1 million. Centenarians, too, are fast becoming more than just oddities: there are now roughly 50,000 Americans 100 years or older. By the year 2050, according to the U.S. Census Bureau, there will be more like a million.

Half of our elderly live in eight states: California, New York, Florida, Pennsylvania, Texas, Illinois, Ohio, and Michigan. Florida, where so many people go to retire, has an elderly population that is higher than the national average: 17.6 percent. Little Rhode Island, smallest of the states, is not far behind: 14.6 percent of its population of 993,000 is sixty-five and older. Two-thirds of the elderly live in metropolitan areas — core cities and surrounding suburbs. In Tampa–St. Petersburg and Fort Lauderdale–Hollywood (all in Florida), more than 20 percent of the residents are over sixty-five.[1] Worldwide, over the past few years most of the elderly have lived in developing countries — and by the beginning of the twenty-first century, they will make up three-fourths of the earth's population. This is so because there has been a marked and steady increase in life expectancies even in the poorest countries of the world. While African nations still lag behind, even there, according to Alexandre Kalache, a consultant to the World Health Organization's Global Programme on the Health of the Elderly, the upward trend in longevity will be followed.[2]

Many elderly Americans live alone — about a third of those over sixty-five who are not in institutions and some 10 percent of those who are more than eighty-five. According to a 1986 survey conducted by Louis Harris and Associates, some eight out of ten of those who live alone are women.[3] The rest live with others — a spouse or an adult child or a relative.

While many elderly people are financially secure, many are not: of those who live alone a quarter have incomes below the federal poverty level of $5,447. Moreover, the number of people living below poverty level varies from state to state, ranging from a low of 10 percent in California to a high of 46 percent in Wyoming.

In two other states, Wisconsin and Missouri, more than 40 percent of the very old are poor.

Most of the elderly have their health-care needs covered by some form of insurance, notably Medicare, the government program that helps those over sixty-five. But for one out of five insurance coverage is restricted to Medicare; these people have no other type of coverage to supplement it. This group of elderly is made up mostly of blacks, the poor, and the very oldest of the old. "Large numbers of older Americans have no financial plan to pay for long-term care," said the Harris survey. "Their unpreparedness results partly from ignorance about their current coverage — and in many cases the mistaken belief that their current insurance such as Medicare will pay for nursing home costs."[4]

While the surveys and statistics alone cannot really tell us who the elderly are — no more than can numbers like sixty-five or seventy-five or eighty — they do show us that "the elderly" are not, despite the commonly held notion, a vast group of individuals who think, behave, and live as one. Old people are as different from one another as you are from your friends. A ninety-year-old in relatively good health looks and feels far younger than someone of comparable age who has suffered a stroke and is confined to a wheelchair. Very old persons living in Maine, Utah, and Vermont probably have had more average years of schooling than their counterparts in Alaska or Hawaii. An old man, as we have indicated, has a better chance of dying before an old woman. Elderly blacks often live far drearier lives than elderly whites do and do not always receive the same health care. Just as women outlive men, so do whites outlive blacks and Americans of other ethnic groups. Although the gap is narrowing (and nonwhite women still outlive white men), white people outlive blacks and other nonwhites by an average of 5.6 years from birth and 1.1 years from age sixty-five. According to some experts, however, though life expectancy differences between the sexes are due largely to differing mortality rates after age sixty-five, the discrepancies between the races may be primarily attributed to mortality differences before age sixty-five. They point out that the mortality rate between the races has actually been narrowing throughout this century.[5]

While we must always be mindful of the differences and inequalities that exist among the aged, we can say with some degree of certainty that the majority of elderly Americans are fairly healthy, active, and mentally alert. Aging does not always mean a journey of emotional and physical deterioration that leads to a nursing home. In fact, there is ample evidence that the majority of elderly people are happy with their lives, and many are well off — just the opposite of what young people generally believe about old folks, that they are poor, sickly, and lonely. Seventy percent of elderly Americans, in fact, report that they are healthy, and three-fourths own their own homes. Aging, according to Dr. T. Franklin Williams, director of the National Institute of Aging, is not what it used to be. "There's no inevitable decline with aging," he said recently. "We have lots of good research data showing that many people live into their 90s in very good health and functioning. Humans who have a reasonably good life style and are fortunate enough not to have one of the major diseases can be essentially as functional in their 80s and 90s as young people."[6]

With all that in mind, a better way of answering the question "Who are the elderly?" is to respond with another question: "Which elderly?"

Here is how psychologist Ken Dychtwald and Mark Zitter, an authority on aging and health care, have addressed the many differences among people far older than you:

The elderly are usually thought of as a group with common attributes. Using general averages and percentages to examine myths about health, wealthy, and mental acuity would seem to imply a similarity among all or most older persons. Yet in reality, people tend to grow more different from one another as they age, making the elderly the most diverse of all age segments. Variation is greater among the elderly than other groups in terms of health, eduction, lifestyle, marital status, physical capabilities, living arrangements, economic well-being, even age itself — no other age group spans 30 plus years. The over-65 age bracket is the only segment that encompasses parents and children from the same family: over ten percent of elderly persons have at least one child age 65 or over.

To enable us to understand better the diversity among older people, Dychtwald and Zitter have subdivided them into three groups.

■ Middle Adulthood (forty through sixty). In this stage, most Americans change their work lives significantly but remain deeply involved in society. Some 48 million Americans — one-fifth of the population — belong to this group.

■ Late Adulthood (sixty through eighty). This is a time of somewhat less activity, although most people in this group are able to care for themselves and stay active. More than 33 million Americans are in this group, accounting for about 14 percent of our population.

■ Old Age (eighty and over). This stage is the one that most of us associate with the dependency and health problems of age. However, the vast majority of people in this category are mentally alert and living in the community. More than 6 million Americans — 2.5 percent of the population — comprise this group.

And what will tomorrow's elderly, a group that includes you and your classmates, be like?

Dychtwald and Zitter believe that it is natural for us to use the elderly of today as a model for the elderly of the future. But this, they argue, is wrong. As they see it:

Tomorrow's elderly will be healthier, wealthier, more mobile, better educated, and more accustomed to change than their predecessors. They will also comprise a larger age [group] that will wield greater political and economic power. . . . Unlike today's older Americans, the elderly of the future will have grown up expecting to live into their 70s, 80s, and beyond.

Tomorrow's elderly will also differ from their predecessors in terms of attitude toward work and retirement. In 1900, the average male spent over two thirds of his life working, but just 1.2 years — three percent of his life — in retirement. By 1980, men on the average were spending just over half of their lives working, but nearly 14 years — 20 percent of their lives — in retirement. Thus, while life expectancy increased by 50 percent, average duration of retirement for men rose over 1100 percent. Women, on the other hand, have become more likely to work outside of the home. Between 1900 and 1980, labor force participation figures for women rose from 6.3 years to 27.5 years and from 13 percent to 36 percent of their average life span. In the future, older persons of both sexes will have experienced both work and retirement.

Differences in eduction also are illustrative of the changes to come. Currently less than half of all persons over age 65 have completed high school, and about one fourth never finished grade school. Fewer than one in ten finished college. In contrast, Americans between the ages of 40 and 60, who will join the ranks of the elderly during the next few decades, have a great deal of formal education.

Three-fourths of this generation completed high school, over one-third attended college, and less than ten percent failed to finish grade school.

Tomorrow's elderly will also have seen dramatic advances in technology, information, and telecommunications. They will have traveled and read more, have experienced more varied people and cultures, and have lived longer than their predecessors. In short, the elderly of the future will be far more accustomed to change than any previous age group in history. Their increased flexibility, awareness, and power, combined with their greater numbers, will transform the role of the elderly in American society.[7]

As a young person, then, you have great advantages over your parents and grandparents. When you are their age, you will not be exactly like them, no matter how easy it is to believe that you will be, no matter how many times you hear the expression, "Wait till you're my age." Certainly, you will share some of the things that your parents and grandparents share with all older people: the responsibilities of a spouse, children, a job; perhaps poor eyesight, a failing memory for events that happened only a few days ago, or gray hair, false teeth, a slower walk. Your face may even resemble theirs to a startling degree, wrinkles and all. But your life in the future will go beyond those badges of aging that have been ours to wear almost since humans first appeared on the earth. What you are experiencing today cannot help but make

you different from your ancestors when you grow old —
just as what your parents experienced made them different from their parents, and your grandparents different from everyone else in their families who came
before. Experiences shape our lives, and because you
have had, or will have, more and varied experiences, the
more you will differ from your less-experienced, less-
mobile, less-informed ancestors.

Isn't it logical to assume that growing up in this tech-
nological and atomic age will shape your views in later
life in ways that are totally unlike the views of a person
who grew up during the American Revolution? If, as a
youth, you have already traveled overseas on a jetliner,
arriving in a foreign country in a few hours, should it
come as any surprise, when you are older, that people
are now traveling to the moon or the planets almost as
easily as you left for another country? I doubt that it will.
You'll probably accept interplanetary travel without raising an eyebrow. By contrast, the youth who grew up
during the Revolution would find it hard enough to
accept routine travel out of the country for pleasure —
let alone in the likes of a plane, or, an even bigger
stretch of the imagination, off of the planet earth aboard
a spaceship!

If you are a young woman, you are certain to be different from your mother when you are old. Many of the
opportunities that were denied her in her generation are
being offered to you today. When your mother was
young, and certainly when your grandmother was, many

women had only homemaking and raising children as a goal. Indeed, there was usually not even a choice. Times are changing for the better. Though women still are not on a fully equal footing with men — they often earn less than men do for performing the very same jobs and may not be promoted as readily — the gap between the sexes is narrowing. This is bound to affect a woman's attitudes when she grows old and the role she will play as a senior citizen.

In all likelihood, you will be in better physical shape than your parents and grandparents are now, and you will be, it is hoped, far more satisfied with your life than they are. One reason for this is that many young people nowadays are showing signs of being more health conscious. If health education does what it is supposed to do —get you to cut out the wrong foods and cigarettes, limit your alcohol intake, and exercise more — there is no doubt that you will live a longer, healthier, and more productive life.

Yes, you will reach old age someday, just as your parents and grandparents did. But though you may look the way they do now and have the same emotions as they do, chances are very good that you won't see the world, its problems, and the best ways to resolve those problems as they do.

Nor will you necessarily age in the same way and at the same rate as your peers. Your family history, and the way you live, will see to that. Perhaps you will even grow up without some of the negative views of aging that have scarred generations of young and old alike. If so, that would be a wonderful thing. What for your elders was sometimes regarded as the worst of times could well turn out to be the best of times when you reach their age.

3 ▪
WHY DO WE AGE?

"It is time to be old,
To take in sail."
— Ralph Waldo Emerson

We age, of course, because . . . not so easy to answer that, is it? Well, we might say that we age simply because, as Emerson said, it is time. Everybody and everything ages, don't they? People, animals, trees, even stones age. If we continue to exist, we eventually grow old. All it takes is the passage of time. An African Bushman once told a visiting anthropologist who had asked him what made him old: "Well, you know, what happens is that time passes. The rain comes, and then the dry season, then it rains again. That's what moves you."[1] It is more complicated than that. The phenomenon of aging is still one of the most complicated mysteries facing biologists today.

To begin with, not all things age in the same way or at the same speed. Boulders and buildings age because weather and pollution gradually wear them away. It may take hundreds of years, maybe thousands in the case of rocks and monuments, but it will happen, and they will not look the way they did when they were younger. But is that really aging? Not in the sense that we apply the process to living things like us. With humans, aging is a bit different. Environmental hazards do assault and affect us, of course, just as they do inanimate objects. Smoke-laden air, acid rain, radiation, the greenhouse effect, intense cold or heat — all of these can injure us, sometimes enough to make us die before our time. The sun can make our skin "age," turning it brown and leathery. We say our hair turns gray because someone or something is worrying us. We become stooped because of years of back-breaking labor.

But this kind of aging, and the sort that causes inanimate objects to age under the influence of an external event, is not *aging* in the biological sense of the word. We merely look old after exposure to the elements or some other natural event. And though we may die prematurely because of some environmental hazard, this does not mean we have aged prematurely and died as a result of aging. Aging in a living creature, what scientists call biological aging, occurs from within, not from without. It appears to be a built-in event, something that very precisely and deliberately limits our life spans. Our cells, it seems, work like clocks that are "wound" at birth and set, or programmed, to run out at a given time. Evidence of that theory comes from observations that identical twins have similar life spans, and that each animal species has a time-measured span. That is why, say the theorists, rabbits live for five or six years, monkeys about fifteen years, and human beings for many years more.

There are many other theories about why we age. Some scientists blame accumulated damage from waste products in our body's cells and molecules over the years. These wastes, some of them poisonous, may progressively destroy our cells. As the cells slowly die, we age. Another theory says that as we grow older, the immune system — the natural barrier we all have against disease — somehow goes wrong and becomes unable to tell the difference between the body it is supposed to defend and a foreign invader, like a germ or a virus. As a result, goes the theory, we attack ourselves from within, mistaking our own bodies for, say, bacteria, and thus slowly destroy the carefully regulated system in our bodies that controls such vital processes as blood pressure, temperature, pulse rate, and the delicate balance of chemicals and hormones. Still another theory says there is a "death gene" in each of us, a gene coded for age that shuts us all down when it is time, when our biological alarm clock sounds.

No matter which of these theories your prefer — and your choice is as good as mine since none has won out yet — it is difficult to avoid the role of the cell. This is because cells, jam-packed with intricate biochemical machinery, are the smallest basic units of life. Cells contain the mechanism that manufactures protein, the material of which all of our organs and, ultimately, we, are made. And they build the defenses against disease in our tissues. When our cells — and the cells of everything that lives, be it a mosquito or a man — stop making protein, the entire structure falls apart and dies. That falling apart is, in a sense, the aging process. It is slow. No one ages suddenly, so forget those movies about people turning old and white-haired an instant after being scared out of their wits by some horrible monster or scary event.

If you've studied biology, you know that cells divide and redivide over and over again to produce identical copies of themselves. New skin cells are generated every day, for instance, to replace others depleted by disease or injury. A look at how fast a scab forms from new cells on a cut finger is proof of that. Our red blood cells renew themselves every few days, the cells in our hearts at a slower rate.

For a long time, scientists thought that because of all of this dividing and redividing cells had the potential for being immortal. If they could be cared for properly, perhaps given some chemical food, they might go on and on forever. One scientist who believed this was Alexis Carrel, a French biologist who won the Nobel prize in 1912. Indeed, Carrel was able to keep some chicken cells growing and multiplying in a laboratory culture dish for some thirty years by feeding them an extract made from chicken embryos. Carrel finally put a stop to his experiment, saying that if he had not thrown out some of his growing cells every day the whole concoction would have covered the earth's surface in twenty years.

Carrel's experiment, if it had worked the way he thought it was working, might have had some important bearing on the quest for a laboratory Fountain of Youth. All we would have to do to keep us alive forever would be to find the right cell food, and perhaps sprinkle it on our breakfast cereals. Our cells would keep on multiplying and churning out new body-building protein as fast as our old cells died off. Unfortunately, there was a flaw in Carrel's experiment. It turned out that the embryo extract he fed his chicken cells contained fresh, living cells, and these were what kept rejuvenating the original culture, keeping it "alive" for so long.

Another celebrated cell culture that led some scientists to speculate that cells had the potential to be immortal is the so-called HeLa Strain. This long-living line of cells had its beginning in 1951 with cells taken from a young woman with cancer. Scientists called her Helen Lane, and the cell line took its name from the first two letters of her first and last names. Not only were the HeLa cells the first human cancer cells to multiply in a culture dish, they continue to do so today. They are dividing and growing in laboratories throughout the world, and are among the hardiest and most studied of human cell strains. Although Helen Lane died of cancer, her cells, ironically, have achieved immortality of a sort.

But does this mean that cells are truly immortal? Not really. The HeLa cells keep on multiplying indefinitely apparently because they are cancerous, and therefore abnormal. Ordinarily, cells contain forty-six chromosomes — threadlike structures made up of genes — twenty-three from each parent. The HeLa cells had up to 350 chromosomes, more than enough to confuse the mechanism that directs the normal rate of cell growth and, at the same time, seemingly slow the biological clock of aging.

The idea that there is such a genetic clock, a timer that puts a limit on how many years we can live, goes back several years. There is, for example, a strange disease known as progeria that provides some evidence for a cellular clock. The disease is a very rare one that afflicts children and causes them to age prematurely. Only about fifteen children in the world are known to have progeria. Kids with the disease look just like very old people. Though they appear normal at birth, by the time they are one year old, they are bald, have loose and wrinkled skin, receding chins, and stunted, stooping growth. Children with progeria generally die on average at sixteen — usually of heart attacks. Scientists who study progeria believe that something amiss in the genes causes these children to age before their time. They reason that because each of the changes that children with progeria undergo are the same ones that occur with normal aging, a genetic clock must be the timekeeper.

It was an American biologist, Leonard Hayflick, who came up with the best evidence for a genetic clock of aging. He did that by taking some cells from the lungs of a four-month-old embryo. When he cultured the cells in his laboratory, he discovered that they doubled about fifty times before dying. But when he removed cells from the lung tissue of a twenty-year-old man, they multiplied only twenty times before they quit. This showed that there was a limit to the doubling process, and that it was somehow related to life span. Next, Dr. Hayflick tried to find out whether the cells could "remember" the number of times they multiplied if their clocks were stopped. To determine that, he froze some of the cells at ten doublings, and some others at twenty doublings. The result was astonishing: when the cells were thawed out, they resumed dividing exactly as many times as they were supposed to according to the doubling program they had followed before their clocks were stopped. For instance, cells that were frozen at twenty doublings went on to divide about thirty more times before they died at fifty. Moreover, the cells managed to take up where they left off even after being frozen for ten years!

Dr. Hayflick also determined that the number of times the cells doubled varied with different species of animals. Mouse cells divided about a dozen times, while those from a chicken, which lives far longer than a mouse, divided about twice as many times. Long-living tortoises had cells that divided up to 125 times. And what of human beings? As Dr. Hayflick noticed when he cultivated the embryo cells in his lab, they doubled about fifty times. This took approximately six months in the laboratory. It is interesting to note that that number of cell doublings, fifty, would take about 115 years to play out within the human body — and 115 years is roughly the longest a human being can expect to live under the best of conditions. Many scientists believe that the doubling limit of fifty holds true in the body as well as in the lab, and that the more points we have in our favor — a long-lived family is one — the better the chances that our cells will reach the maximum number of doublings.

But one must understand that the fifty doublings represent the ultimate limit that a human can reach. We do not live long enough now — certainly the majority of us do not — to enjoy the maximum number of cell doublings. (In the case of children with progeria, it is interesting to note that their cells do not divide more than ten times. It is as though the cells had quickly lived out the forty or so doublings that an old cell would have experienced.) Dr. Hayflick has emphasized that his observation is only an example of aging at the cellular level rather than its cause. "Cell division is only one cell process," he says. "I don't believe cells or human beings die because cells stop dividing, but from functional changes that occur before cell division stops."[2] Thus, although it is tempting to believe that we age just because our cells quit doubling, it is probably true that we experience various age changes that take the power out of our cells well before that.

Now it is true that scientists do not always agree. All one has to do to understand that is go to a scientific meeting. After a speaker has presented evidence for one theory or other, there are almost always questions from the audience — and criticism. Someone says he or she did the very same experiment, and came up with just the opposite result. Another challenges the method by which the experiment was conducted. Still another might simply be unkind, for despite the friendly atmosphere that generally seems to revolve around scientists you may see portrayed in television movies, such is not always the case. The point is, science is still a never-ending quest, and no one has all the answers, least of all when it comes to why we age. Not all scientists believe that mortality is programmed into our cells, and to argue their point they cite cases where cell lines have been kept alive for a very long time with drugs and vitamins. They will tell you that not all of the tissues of our bodies age at the same rate, that indeed some cells may be programmed to die before the whole person dies. They will also call your attention to the fact that one-celled organisms — critters like yeast, algae, bacteria, and amoebas — seem to have no preset life spans. They divide and redivide, forever, it seems, until something kills them. Why shouldn't we be able to do the same?

We cannot yet answer that question. What we can say is that there seems to be no one mechanism for aging, be it a single death-dealing gene or some other master clock somewhere in our bodies. It appears that many body systems are involved in aging, and that many centers and many different genes control it. It also seems that instead of spending so much time trying to find out why we age and how to arrest the aging process, we should focus on improving the lives of the growing numbers of elderly people. It is the quality of life that is important.

4 ■
PHYSICAL AILMENTS OF THE ELDERLY

"What a drag it is getting old."
— Mick Jagger and Keith Richards

Old age isn't always a drag, but neither is it always pleasant. Some of the less than upbeat views of aging you read in the first chapter are often based on fact. People do grow old and they do incur a lot of problems. If you know about and understand these problems, perhaps then you will be able to recognize them when you, too, are aged. And you may realize why some old people behave the way they do. That may keep you from growing impatient with your elderly grandmother or crotchety great-uncle when she or he seems to be totally out of touch with you and your attitudes.

It should not be too difficult to show some compassion for an old person who seems gruff if you consider that something heavy might be weighing on his or her mind. Perhaps your grandfather has an ailment that frightens him. Perhaps your grandmother is depressed over losses that occurred in her life long before you were born. Or the old people you encounter may be bitter about lost opportunities. They feel cheated, and maybe they envy you your youth — youth that gives you the time to do the things they wish they had done. Sometimes, too, elderly people don't always hear or remember what you've just said and may give vague or unenthusiastic answers to some of your questions. That sort of response can easily be taken as an indication that they don't care and force you to conclude that they act strangely just because they are old.

But you should remember that there are always reasons behind someone's anger or distant behavior. Many times these have little to do with old age. Try not to take an elderly person's touchiness personally. Instead, try to see matters from his or her perspective. Ask yourself how you would respond if you weren't feeling well and a friend began making demands on your time. Would you be happy about that? Think how you would react to a friend's bubbling over with enthusiasm about a stroke of good fortune when you were in the pits. Would you find it easy to be interested, let alone excited? Consider how it must be to have experienced several times over the things someone else is experiencing for the first time. Could you be enthusiastic? Probably not; chances are you'd also be bored. And you'd probably become irritated because you couldn't have those experiences again. Often an old person's irritability stems from frustration, from some problem unresolved or some need unfulfilled. It is better for you to try to ignore the surface aspects of an old person's peculiar behavior and focus instead on what may be in back of it.

Here are some things you need to know. Aging makes a person susceptible to a wide variety of physical and mental problems. This doesn't mean that all old people are automatically doomed to ill health and suffering, nor that aging itself causes disease. The illnesses that the elderly get are often caused by many other things. And many manage to live long lives in fairly good health.

Still, it cannot be denied that as we get older changes occur in the body. In one's twenties, for example, the production of hormones begins to slow up. Hormones are body chemicals that regulate just about everything from one's personality to sexual behavior to how fast the heart beats. Shifts in hormone levels mean both physical and emotional changes. By the time one is in one's thirties, the heart is not pumping blood as easily, and the lungs, linked by arteries to the heart, will not receive as much oxygen as they once did. In one's eighties, the slowup is even more evident: by that time, the amount of blood pumped by the heart each minute has decreased by 30 to 40 percent.

When one is a baby, the pulse rate is about 130 beats a minute; at sixty, it will be 67 to 80. As the clock ticks on, the kidneys and the bladder won't function as efficiently as they did, one's arteries will be less resilient, fat deposits will increase around the heart, and body temperature will be lower. Breathing capacity by the time a person reaches fifty is down to 75 percent of the original capacity, as the lungs become less flexible and the muscles that control breathing weaken. What doctors call the basal metabolic rate — the speed at which we expend energy while at rest — decreases. An older person's skin is not as tight as a youth's, especially under the eyes and chin, and his or her hearing and eyesight are not as sharp. The sense of taste is less keen in the elderly: a thirty-year-old, for instance, has more than half again the number of taste buds — sensor cells in the tongue and mouth — than an eighty-year-old has.

With increasing age, one becomes shorter and probably stooped. Bones turn brittle and lighter as they lose calcium, muscles shrink and become weaker, and thus they affect not only the way one works, plays, and breathes, but even the way one goes to the bathroom. Most important, the brain grows smaller and lighter as each day thousands of its cells die and aren't replaced. By the time one reaches seventy, the brain will be about half of what it once was. Eventually, it may be clogged with cellular debris or lose vital chemicals — changes that can rob a person of his or her memory and can cause disordered behavior and many of the other distressing mental changes we associate with old age.

It sounds pretty gloomy. Bodies grow old and parts wear out, so to speak. But many of these changes are reasonably easily coped with. One can wear eyeglasses or a hearing aid to bolster those weakening senses. Proper nutrition can overcome deficiencies; exercise can strengthen muscles and improve the condition of the heart and blood vessels; hormones can be replaced. A facelift can tighten the sagging jowls and remove bags under the eyes. None of these things will *remake* one's body, but they will help perk it up and perhaps keep it in fairly good condition.

But aging does bring with it some serious health problems, diseases that prevent or limit an older person from functioning normally, both physically and mentally. Overall, old people usually need more medical attention than the young do and often develop several disorders at the same time. Many of the ailments are chronic — that is, they are lingering problems or diseases that usually are difficult, if not impossible, to cure. That is why the quality of life of many old people suffers and why they often must become dependent on others. The ailing elderly can also place emotional stress on families who must care for them, and a financial strain both on the families and on the various agencies that must help pay for their health care. Society in general loses, too, because many of the elderly would still be able to perform productive work if they weren't ill. Indeed, studies indicate that 45 percent of elderly men and 35 percent of elderly women cannot carry on major activities because of poor health.

Some of the diseases and other problems that afflict the elderly are well understood and can be treated; others defy understanding but still can be treated. Still others are not understood well and are untreatable. Because both chronic and acute (short-lived and severe, as opposed to long-drawn-out) diseases are prevalent among the elderly, you should know something about them — both for the sake of those elderly people you may know and for your own.

ARTHRITIS

If there is one disease most often associated with being old, it is this ailment. Known as the "great crippler," it can strike people in their twenties, thirties, and forties, and even children, but it is by far the most common chronic condition that limits an older person's activities. The word *arthritis* comes from the Greek words *arth*, meaning joint, and *itis*, meaning inflammation. The disease is exactly that. People who have it suffer pain and swelling in various joints — knees, hips, spine, ankles, knuckles — and joints are often deformed. Inflammation is one way the body reacts to an injury or disease. When there is an injury or an infection, the body's natural defense, its immune system, begins to repair the damage. In an injured joint, this repair process causes swelling, pain, and stiffness, usually temporary conditions — except in arthritic joints. Age is definitely a factor in arthritis: according to some authorities, a person over sixty-five has an 80 percent higher chance of developing the disease than someone of middle age. As many as 36 million people in the United States have some form of arthritis (there are more than one hundred related disorders, all of them, arthritis included, coming under the name rheumatic diseases). Most forms cannot be cured, and the underlying causes are not fully understood.

Some 16 million Americans have the most common kind, osteoarthritis, a degenerative disorder that attacks individual joints and is the result of the normal wear and tear that comes with age. It generally affects the large weight-bearing joints — hip, knee, and lower back. Osteoarthritis can begin early in life if a joint is injured in an accident, or overused in, say, strenuous sports. It may also occur in an overweight person because the extra weight puts enormous strain on the joints. In osteoarthritis, the smooth material called cartilage that covers the bone ends of a joint becomes rough and wears away. Sometimes an abnormal bone growth, or spur, develops, causing great pain.

Another form is rheumatoid arthritis. This is a chronic inflammatory disease whose cause is not yet known. It is a so-called systemic disease — that is, it can affect many parts of the body as well as the joints. In this form, chemicals in the joint fluid — joints contain a sort of lubricant that helps reduce friction as we move — attack the lining of the joint and damage it. According to the American Academy of Orthopaedic Surgeons, more than 70 percent of the people with rheumatoid arthritis are over thirty years old. The disease peaks in men between the ages of sixty and sixty-nine, and in women (who have more rheumatoid arthritis than men) between fifty and fifty-nine.

Gout is another, very painful, form of arthritis that can afflict the elderly. It is caused when a chemical defect in the body forces another naturally occurring chemical, uric acid, to build up. Uric acid is usually disposed of in the urine, but when too much of it stays behind it can form crystals that stick in the joints, often in the big toe, and cause them to swell.

Treatment of arthritis is aimed at lessening pain and trying to improve the function of the diseased joints. Aspirin and other anti-inflammatory drugs are often used, and sometimes a sufferer gets shots of a substance called cortisone to bring down the swelling. Often, surgery is required to remove the damaged joint lining, change the position of joints, or replace joints with artificial ones.

If you're trying to help older people with arthritis, there's not much you can do — except possibly to remind them to take their medicine. Some old people forget to do so, and drugs that control inflammation must be taken regularly to get the most benefit from them. But there are some other things you can do to help. It is most important for a person with arthritis, especially osteoarthritis, to keep the joints mobile. That is why many therapists advise arthritis sufferers to do daily, gentle exercises that relieve stiffness and strengthen the muscles around the joints. You can help your arthritic grandmother by learning more about the specific exercises that have been prescribed and encouraging her to do them. These usually are fairly simple routines that teach a person to move various joints through their full range of motion and to stand and sit properly. Or, since walking is good exercise for a person with arthritis, you could take your grandmother on regular walks. If she needs extra assistance, such as a cane, crutches, or a walker, and is reluctant to use a prop, you just might be the one person to convince her that a cane is often as necessary as your eyeglasses and is nothing to be ashamed of.

Older people with arthritis also need help performing those everyday tasks that younger people take for granted: dressing, eating, writing, cooking. You can keep your eyes out for simple devices that can make an elderly person less dependent on other people. Things like long-handled shoehorns, combs, and kitchen utensils make practical and inexpensive gifts; you can also buy clothes without buttons or complicated snaps that even a person with swollen hands and stiff fingers can get into easily. Treating arthritis involves more people than just the person with the disease and his or her doctor. The National Institute of Arthritis and Musculoskeletal and Skin Diseases puts it this way: "No factor is more important in the treatment and rehabilitation of the arthritis patient than maintenance of psychological balance under the stressful conditions imposed by the disease. Complex emotional and vocational problems resulting from chronic disability often require the attention of psychologists, social workers, and vocational specialists. In the overall management of arthritis, these specialists must work in close cooperation with each other and with the doctors, therapists, relatives of the patient and others involved if best results are to be achieved."[1] If you are interested in learning more about arthritis, you can write to the Institute at Building 31, Room 4CO5, Bethesda, Maryland 20892, or to the Arthritis Foundation, 2045 Peachtree Road, N.E., Atlanta, Georgia 30339–1405.

ACCIDENTS

It is no wonder that elderly people who begin to have difficulty seeing and hearing, and whose reflexes are not as sharp as they once were, can make errors in judgment. Because their reaction time is often off, or because they are weakened by some muscular disorder, they may be more prone to accidents on the road or in the home than a younger person is.

Older drivers, for example, may easily be disoriented by shifts in light or weather conditions or may not be able to react fast enough when traffic patterns change suddenly. Sometimes, if their hands and elbows are arthritic, they may have trouble turning a steering wheel promptly. Automobile accidents, of course, can happen to younger people as well. Young drivers show a lot of poor judgment when behind the wheel, and those under the age of twenty are generally involved in more accidents than are older drivers — but the causes are not the same. Young drivers are impetuous and speedy; older drivers are slow and cautious in their responses. According to a 1988 study by the Transportation Research Board and the National Research Council, elderly drivers ranked second only to sixteen-to-twenty-four-year-olds in the number of accidents per mile driven. Another study found that drivers seventy-five and older were more accident-prone than all other drivers except those under twenty-five.[2] (The statistics may be a little misleading, since older citizens drive fewer miles than do younger drivers.) Many automobile accidents involving the elderly are fatal: a fourth of the accidental deaths among old people in one year are attributed to motor vehicles, and nearly half of these deaths in people over the age of seventy-five involve pedestrians.

Because of the physical changes that come with aging, several states have passed laws requiring elderly drivers to take special tests in order to get their licenses renewed. But such measures are not especially popular with those who feel strongly that singling out the elderly for license renewals contributes to age discrimination. Said Dr. Thomas Planek, director of research and statistical services at the National Safety Council in Chicago, "The use of age as an indicator of poor driving is simply not supportable. There are no absolutes of old age."[3] Also, the use of an automobile is important to many older people who need cars not only to get around more easily but also to maintain their spirit of independence. Driving keeps elderly people connected to the neighborhood and to other places where friends and family live, something that is especially desirable since many old people live alone.

Someday, if it has not already happened, your parents — the same people you used to argue with about using the family car — will seem to you to be a little too shaky to get behind the wheel. Perhaps, when one of them is driving and you're sitting in the front seat, you will notice that he or she is making turns too wide or too short, or failing to yield the right of way to another driver. It's quite natural for you to be concerned, even afraid. But it is important that you not express your dismay too strongly. For one thing, your parents might become angry because their authority is being challenged — after all, they're supposed to tell *you* what to do. For another, your nagging over their frightening driving habits could heighten any anxiety they may already feel over growing old: when elderly people keep hearing people tell them that they aren't as sharp as they once were, they can easily get depressed. For those reasons, it is best that you not demand that they quit driving altogether. Instead, you might suggest that they not drive when it's raining, or at night. You could look for a driver-refresher course in the neighborhood and enroll your parents in it. Or, if you are old enough to have a license, you might act as a driving instructor yourself, possibly using the excuse that rules and conditions have changed and that you'd like to share some of the new things you have been taught about safe driving. As Dr. James Malfetti, director of the Safety Research and Education Project at Columbia University, has put it:

"Elderly drivers are pretty good at self-regulation. Once they become aware of their limitations, they will make adjustments."[4] A few years ago, Britain's oldest driver, John Meldrum, drove until he was 101 years of age. He called it quits after he had his first accident — a minor fender-bender — after a million miles of motoring. Meldrum's attitude when he turned in his license was realistic. "When you're over a hundred," he said, "and your eyesight is not what it used to be, and your legs are not as strong, it's time to give up."[5]

The elderly are sometimes in as much danger at home as on the road. Probably the most common risk for them is that of falling. According to Dr. Rein Tideiksaar, director of the Falls and Immobility Program at the Mount Sinai Medical Center Jewish Home and Hospital for the Aged in New York City, every year approximately 30 to 50 percent of people sixty-five and older who do not live in institutions suffer from falls. Falls are the leading cause of accidental death and the sixth most common cause of death among people seventy-five and older; half of all people over the age of sixty-five who are hospitalized for falls and their resulting complications are dead within a year.[6]

There are many reasons why old people fall and injure themselves. Fluctuations in blood pressure, strokes that cut the blood supply to the brain, and weakened bones are some of them. Certain medicines may make an elderly person dizzy, as can overexertion and failure to take some prescribed medicines. Some old people may even deny that they are getting along in years, and this denial makes them careless about how they walk or climb up and down stairs or step onto an icy sidewalk.

One of the most serious results of a fall in an elderly person is a hip fracture. According to Dr. Tideiksaar, between $1 billion and $2 billion are spent every year on hospitalization costs of repairing hip fractures alone. And that enormous amount doesn't include the cost of emergency room visits, trips to the doctor, rehabilitation, and other services. Nor does it take into account the cost of disability, treatment of secondary complications, medicines and loss of productivity. In 1980, some 270,000 hip fractures occurred in the United States, the largest percentage affecting the elderly, especially women; researchers predict that there will be more than 500,000 such fractures a year by the year 2000.[7]

One of the reasons older people are more susceptible to hip fractures is a condition that is common among them, osteoporosis. This disease breaks down old bone tissue faster than the body can manufacture new, healthy tissue, and the result is a wasting away, or thinning, of the bones. There are many causes. One is a diet low in calcium, the metallic element found in milk, cheese, and other foods. Osteoporosis can also occur when a person is immobilized for a long time, as might be the case after a fracture or surgery. Sometimes hormone imbalances can start the disease. The most common cause, however, seems to be the aging process itself. Elderly white women are especially at risk: more than 8 million suffer from osteoporosis in the United States. Hormone and calcium supplements in the diet and exercise are part of the treatment, but prevention of a fall is just as important. You can help elderly people avoid falls by paying attention to the obvious: see to it that they have canes if they are unsteady on their feet, that their homes are well-lighted, and that loose rugs and other hazards that could trip them are removed. You might also think ahead to the day when you, too, should begin to pay more attention to your body than you do now. "I think that in the future we will see a much greater emphasis on early detection of calcium deficiencies," says Dr. Samuel Doppelt, an orthopedic surgeon (one who treats ailments of the muscles, bones, and joints) at the Massachusetts General Hospital. "Like hypertension, conditions such as osteoporosis start off as basically silent disorders. By learning of a calcium deficiency at the age of thirty-five or forty and taking an appropriate supplement, bone loss and the problems associated with it in later life might be avoided."[8]

EYESIGHT

"The light of the body is the eye," says Saint Matthew in his gospel. In the elderly, quite often that light dims or goes out completely. While poor eyesight can strike at any age, the fact remains that more than half of the blind people in America are over sixty-five years old. Eye diseases, it seems, occur more frequently as people age.

According to the American Medical Association, a sixty-year-old person needs seven times as much light as a twenty-year-old to see well. Not a very comforting statistic considering that sight is regarded as the most important of our five main senses. Several disorders contribute to poor vision among the elderly. Probably the one you've heard about most often is cataracts. A cataract occurs when the normally clear lens of the eye — a transparent, oval body that allows the eye to focus on near and far objects — deteriorates with age and becomes cloudy. Both eyes are generally affected, and when cataracts form vision is reduced. People are more likely to develop cataracts as a natural consequence of aging, but certain diseases, diabetes among them, can also cause cataracts. Cataracts tend to run in families, which means you are more likely to get them if a relative is affected. And, if you think that they come only with age you should be aware that sometimes they are present at birth or show up shortly afterward. Often, people with cataracts can get by for a while with glasses, but the only real treatment for severe cases in an operation that removes the lens or some of the material inside it. A plastic lens may be inserted in the eye in place of the real lens, but eyeglasses or contact lenses are more generally worn after the operation.

Another eye disorder that runs in families and often affects the elderly is glaucoma. More than a million Americans over age sixty-five have this disease in which a circulating eye fluid, the aqueous humor, builds up in the eye. The resulting pressure impairs the blood supply to the retina — the light-sensitive, innermost layer of the eyeball — and the optic nerve, both of which enable us to see. Untreated, glaucoma leads to permanent and complete blindness. Eyedrops and other medicines are generally used to cut down the production of fluid and reduce pressure, and they must be taken for life.

Elderly people with vision problems need help from you as well as from professionals. Again, some of what you can do may be obvious but worth mentioning anyway: assist them in walking, get them large-type newspapers or books, or read to them if their vision is seriously impaired.

DIABETES

Diabetes is a disease you've probably heard about a lot because it affects people your age as well as the elderly. There are several types, but each is generally characterized by the inability of the body either to produce a vital and powerful hormone called insulin, or to use it properly. Insulin, secreted by the pancreas, regulates the amount of blood sugar, known as glucose, that your body needs for energy. When there is no insulin, or when it is not used properly, glucose accumulates in the blood and cannot provide energy. People with diabetes usually have symptoms that include excessive thirst, hunger, weight loss, and frequent urination. Moreover, people who have had diabetes for many years often develop serious complications such as heart disease, lessened blood flow to the legs and feet, high blood pressure, stroke, blindness, and kidney failure.

One form of diabetes is called Type I. About a million

Americans have this kind, which is also known as juvenile onset diabetes because it shows up most often during childhood and early adolescence. Type I is the most serious form of diabetes; people with it produce little or no insulin and have to take daily injections of it for life just to survive.

Type II is the most common form of diabetes, affecting 10 million Americans, half of whom are not aware they have the disease. It usually strikes after the age of forty-five, typically in people who are overweight. Type II diabetes is 33 percent higher among blacks and three times higher among Hispanics, compared with the general population; 20 percent of American Indians have the disease. A person with Type II diabetes continues to produce insulin, but cannot utilize it properly. This form is usually treated with diet, drugs that lower blood sugar, and exercise; some people with the disease need daily insulin injections.

A family history of diabetes, along with obesity, increases one's risk of developing the disease. The risk also increases with age. Diabetes, in fact, has been described as a disease of "accelerated aging." According to the American Diabetes Association, nearly 3.1 million people over age sixty-five had diabetes in 1987, and 26,000 diabetic patients over sixty-five were in nursing homes.

Diet is vitally important in the management of diabetes. Like driving habits that may become dangerous, eating the wrong foods can harm a diabetic. But getting an elderly person to change his or her long-established eating habits is sometimes difficult. If you want to help your elderly diabetic grandparents, you could give them a cookbook that has recipes with reduced amounts of sugar or that call for artificial sweeteners. Smaller portions of food should be served to a diabetic because the larger the portion the higher the blood sugar will rise. Because diets have to be tailored to each patient's particular needs, it is important that you be informed about what the nutrition counselor has advised. You should not on your own suggest that a diabetic include or exclude certain foods until you are sure which ones are permitted and which forbidden.

Most diabetics can drink alcohol safely if they are careful to limit how much they drink. On the other hand, alcohol contains so-called empty calories, calories that put on weight but have none of the vitamins, minerals, and other nutrients essential to good health. Alcohol can also raise the levels of fats in the blood, fats that increase one's risk of heart disease — a risk a diabetic already has. Proper nutrition is important, and that includes limiting the foods, like those high in fats, that contribute to heart disease. Weight control is important because losing even five to ten pounds can help the body produce enough insulin to hold blood sugar levels in check.

Exercise combined with diet can control diabetes. Not only does exercise use up unwanted calories, it also makes the body more sensitive to insulin, thus enabling a diabetic to lower blood sugar levels. Regular exercise, too, reduces some of the risk of heart disease by lowering the amount of cholesterol, a fatty substance found in the body and in foods like eggs and meat that has been strongly linked to heart disease. Only a doctor should prescribe the exact amount of exercise an elderly diabetic should do, but you can help encouraging your grandparents to exercise properly and regularly. Above all, bear in mind that diabetes is a disease that calls for daily attention. Sometimes the elderly people who have diabetes grow tired of having to do something like exercise every single day or be careful of their diet. In cases like that, you can do a lot to lessen their feelings of boredom and being alone simply by being there when they need you.

For more information on diabetes, you can contact the American Diabetes Association National Service Center, 1660 Duke Street, P.O. Box 25757, Alexandria, Virginia 22314.

CARDIOVASCULAR DISEASES

Cardiovascular diseases affect the heart and blood vessels. They are the number one killer in America: in 1987, according to the American Heart Association, cardiovascular diseases killed nearly a million Americans, nearly as many as cancer, accidents, pneumonia, influenza, and all other causes of death combined. Of the current U.S. population of about 250 million, some 66 million suffer from some form of cardiovascular disease.

It is important to know that cardiovascular diseases strike not just the very old. In fact, every year about

200,000 victims of heart and blood vessel diseases are under the age of sixty-five. Moreover, according to a 1989 study, about 60 million Americans twenty years of age and above — about a quarter of the population — need medical help to lower high levels of cholesterol. That means that diet changes, and perhaps drugs that lower cholesterol, are not meant just for the elderly.[9]

Although young people can suffer from heart disease, it is the elderly who are particularly susceptible. One reason is that with age, the amount of blood pumped by the heart decreases. Each day, the normal young heart beats approximately 100,000 times — in a seventy-year lifetime that amounts to more than 2.5 billion beats — and pumps close to 2,000 gallons of blood. Pretty remarkable considering that the heart is a lump of muscle a little bigger than a fist. But the efficiency of a human heart drops from 100 percent during youth to 80 percent by age fifty, to 70 percent by age eighty. Blood pressure — the force exerted by the blood against the blood-vessel walls as the heart pumps — tends to rise with age. Also, blood vessels thicken and lose their normal elasticity, and muscle fibers begin to break down. Atherosclerosis — a disease in which fatty deposits, called plaque, form within the arteries and clog them — is a common cardiovascular disease that generally comes on to some extent by mid-life.

Coronary artery disease, another cardiovascular disease, is caused by atherosclerosis, as is stroke, which occurs when a blood clot blocks a major blood vessel in the brain. Coronary artery disease, the most common cause of cardiovascular death and disability in the United States, results in angina (intense pain caused by a decreased flow of blood to the heart) and heart attacks. Heart attacks occur because the supply of blood to a part of the heart muscle is seriously reduced or blocked completely by some obstruction in the coronary arteries, the arteries that supply blood to the heart muscle. You should know that 55 percent of all heart attack victims are age sixty-five or older, and that of those who die, four out of five are over sixty-five.

While you should never try to diagnose cardiovascular problems in the elderly people you know — certainly the information in this chapter is far too sketchy for that purpose — you can watch for some of the symptoms and risk factors and encourage an elderly person to see a doctor if you're concerned.

High blood pressure, which greatly increases the risk of stroke and other cardiovascular diseases, is one condition you should be aware of. More than 60 million American adults and children have this disease, called hypertension, with blacks at higher risk: they have a 33 percent greater chance of having high blood pressure than whites. Unfortunately, high blood pressure doesn't have very specific symptoms — it is called the silent killer — but a simple, painless test can detect it easily. Blood pressure, especially in the elderly, should be checked at least once a year. You should encourage your parents or grandparents to have the test regularly, especially if they are overweight. If the condition is present, it can be treated with a low-salt diet and/or exercise and weight reduction, restriction of the amount of alcohol that is drunk, and drugs that lower blood pressure.

Getting the elderly person with a cardiovascular disease to stick with whatever treatment program is prescribed is important. You could also become what the Heart Association calls a heart-saver. Among other things, this involves knowing the signs of a heart attack and acting immediately if the signs last two minutes or longer. While all of the warning signs may not occur — and some may indicate another problem — here are the general danger signals:

■ Uncomfortable pressure, fullness, squeezing, or pain in the center of the chest.

■ Pain spreading to the shoulder, neck, and arms.

■ Severe pain, dizziness, sweating, fainting, nausea, or shortness of breath.

If any of these symptoms occur, act quickly because any time lost can be life-threatening or, at least, can increase the risk of major damage to the heart. Call the 911 telephone number for emergency service or get the victim to the nearest hospital emergency room. If you're properly trained, you can give CPR (mouth-to-mouth breathing and chest compression). Being a heart-saver also means learning the risk factors of heart disease, like high blood pressure and increasing age. You should also know that elderly men have a greater risk of heart attack than women. This doesn't mean that elderly women are immune: heart attack is still the leading cause of death among American women. There are other risk factors. Ask whether there is a history of heart disease in your family; this knowledge will affect you as well as your aging parents. Do your elderly grandparents smoke cigarettes? This is important because smokers have more than twice the risk of heart attack as nonsmokers. Moreover, a smoker who has a heart attack is more likely to die from it and more likely to do so suddenly, that is, within an hour. Try to persuade the elderly people you know to cut down or quit, and show them an example by not starting, or quitting yourself. Diabetes, obesity, physical inactivity, and life stress are also risk factors. Being aware of them all can help the elderly people you know live longer. For more information on heart disease, you can write to the American Heart Association's National Center, 7320 Greenville Avenue, Dallas, Texas 75231.

PARKINSON'S DISEASE

You may have noticed that the hands of some elderly people tremble when they hold a glass. Or they may seem unsteady on their feet or walk with a strange, shuffling gait. Sometimes they are forgetful and get lost easily when returning home from a walk. A number of conditions may be responsible for such symptoms, but one of the most common in later life is a disorder called Parkinson's disease. It generally hits people in their sixties, and affects about 5 percent of the population over age sixty-five. Many people with the disease must go to nursing homes because they often cannot wash, dress, or feed themselves.

The cause of Parkinson's disease is not fully known. It is classified as a neurologic disease, that is, one that involves the body's nervous system, the vast network that includes the brain, the spinal cord, and all of the nerves that fan out through our bodies. Among other things, the nervous system enables us to move our muscles by carrying electrical impulses, or messages, from the brain to muscle fibers. The speed at which these nerve impulses travel from the brain to a muscle or organ decreases somewhat with age. Various structural changes also occur inside the brain as a person grows older. Although no one can tell which elderly persons will develop Parkinson's disease, researchers do know that the disease involves various degenerative changes in certain parts of the brain. There is also an imbalance of two chemicals normally present in the brain. These chemicals, called neurotransmitters, transmit the messages between nerve cells.

Treatment for Parkinson's disease involves drugs to restore the balance of brain chemicals, but the drugs are powerful and must be prescribed and monitored by specialists. The drugs do not cure the disease, but doctors tell us that patients can improve, provided they have the will to do so and the help of relatives and friends. As in so many disorders that plague the elderly, exercise and physical therapy are important companions to medicine. Exercise helps strengthen a Parkinson patient's muscles, and doctors recommend a program that includes such activities as walking, stretching, even squeezing a rubber ball. You might assist in these, and perhaps even give an elderly person with the disease a massage from time to time to loosen up stiffened muscles. For further information you can write to the Parkinson's Disease Association of America, 116 John Street, New York, New York 10038.

ALZHEIMER'S DISEASE

You've probably heard a lot more about this disorder than Parkinson's disease, with which it shares the symptom of forgetfulness. But unlike Parkinson's disease, Alzheimer's disease is a major killer: it is the fourth leading cause of death among the elderly. In 1988, more than 100,000 Americans died of the disease, which afflicts an estimated 2.5 million in the United States alone.

Alzheimer's disease generally affects people between the ages of forty-five and sixty-five (people in their twenties have also been diagnosed with it) and is the leading cause of dementia — what we usually refer to as senility — among the elderly. More than 20 percent of people over the age of seventy-five reportedly have the disease.

This disease has been called the "death of the mind." It is no wonder, when you consider what it is capable of. Caused by a progressive degeneration of brain cells that disrupts the transmission of electrochemical messages and eventually erodes all mental and intellectual functions, the disease leads to a chilling list of problems: failing memory and judgment, loss of concentration, changes in personality and behavior, mood swings, depression, agitation, inability to recognize and identify people and objects, and difficulty in walking, talking, and eating. People with Alzheimer's disease may forget the names of close friends and relatives, or what they've read in a newspaper or book only moments ago. Sometimes they forget that a spouse or a parent has died and inquire as to their whereabouts. They may not recall the name of the President of the United States or where they worked. They repeat questions that have been answered, stop in mid-sentence and stare at their feet; they are unable to do simple addition and subtraction or tell time; they have temper tantrums, become suddenly withdrawn, or start to wander aimlessly throughout the house or neighborhood. Eventually, people who suffer from Alzheimer's disease lose all of their connections to the outside world. They become susceptible to other disease and, as the brain is slowly destroyed, they die. The brains of elderly people with Alzheimer's cut open after death reveal tangles of nerve cell fibers and deposits of sticky, clogging substances called senile plaque.

Unfortunately, Alzheimer's disease cannot be detected in its early stages, and it cannot be prevented. While some drugs may be used to treat symptoms like depression and agitation, there are no medications that can reverse the disease itself once it has gained a foothold. People with the disease need twenty-four-hour care, and the psychological and financial strain that this places on families of victims — nursing home care can cost an average of $20,000 per patient a year — can be enormous.

Obviously, not everyone over sixty-five who forgets where he or she parked the car or misplaces articles of clothing has Alzheimer's disease. The majority, in fact, do not. Many other diseases can cause people to become forgetful, and until Alzheimer's disease is diagnosed by a doctor one should not jump to any conclusions. Moreover, occasional forgetfulness isn't necessarily a sign of disease. Says Dr. John Morris, a neurologist at the Washington University School of Medicine, "If the memory loss represents a change in normal behavior, if it seems to get progressively worse, and if it interferes with everyday performance to the point that a spouse, family member or close friend notices it, then it may be a sign that something's wrong and that a visit to a neurologist or other physician familiar with the disease is in order."[10]

When Alzheimer's disease is found in one of your elderly relatives or friends, is there anything you can do? Again, there is no treatment and no cure. But you might be able to make a small difference by staying in touch with the person, by seeing to it that routine daily physical activity is maintained insofar as possible. Because Alzheimer's victims do not take easily to sudden changes, try to keep things pretty much the way they always were. However, you might emphasize some of the things that the patient needs to orient himself or herself. For example, you might put extra calendars around the house, or a few more clocks, perhaps with large digital numbers. Night lights at the doors of the bathroom, bedroom, and kitchen may help keep a disoriented person on track. And again, you have to practice patience. Here's how Leonore Powell, aging specialist at the College of New Rochelle in New York, describes the difficulty in caring for a memory-impaired patient: "Consider that our familiar world has become strange and perhaps threatening to the person with brain damage who cannot manage to react in an ordinary way to an ordinary situation. Simplify, simplify, simplify, as you would for a brain-injured child. Consistent behavior is important. Do your best to contain your fears and your desire to shout or pout. If your relative overreacts or has an angry outburst, don't try to argue or to reason logically. Maintain a quiet, deliberate facade (despite your inner fears or rage), take several deep breaths and try to pacify and mollify your upset relative. Take his hand gently and speak softly. When his overreaction has subsided, do whatever you need to do (talk to a friend, meditate, get some exercise) to relieve your own frustration and sadness."[11]

CANCER

Cancer is not one but a large collection of diseases with a common trait: the wild growth and spread of abnormal cells. While many cancers can be treated and cured if detected early enough, they often result in death if they continue to spread uncontrolled throughout the body. The chilling statistics attest to the seriousness of cancer. In 1989, according to the American Cancer Society, around a million people will be diagnosed with cancer, and 502,000 will die. That amounts to 1,375 people a day, one every sixty-three seconds. Of every five deaths from all causes in the United States, one is from cancer. About 76 million Americans now living will eventually have the disease — about 30 percent, according to present rates. Over the years, cancer will strike in approximately three out of four families.

Given such numbers, you undoubtedly know people who have cancer. Chances are you even know people your own age with the disease. Cancer, in fact, kills more children three to fourteen years of age than any other disease. But cancer has also been called the disease of old age because its incidence and death rate increase significantly as one grows older. More than half of all the cancer diagnosed today occurs in people sixty-five and older. The reason is that cancer often takes several years to develop. Because people live longer nowadays they thus have more chance of getting the disease.

Several cancers are more prevalent among older people. One of these is cancer of the colon and rectum. The colon is the body's large bowel, the lower five to six feet of intestine. At its end is the rectum, which expels waste matter from the body. More than 90 percent of people diagnosed with colon cancer in 1988 were over fifty, and more than 50,000 people died in 1988 from cancers of the colon and rectum. Treatment sometimes involves removal of the affected part of the bowel; sometimes the surgery is combined with radiation therapy, which, in effect, bombards the cancer cells with rays that destroy them. Drugs — cancer drugs are collectively referred to as chemotherapy — may also be used to kill the cancer cells.

Common among elderly men is prostate cancer, which killed some 28,000 men in 1989. The prostate is a chestnut-sized gland located in the abdomen below the bladder that supplies fluid for semen, the secretion that contains the male reproductive cells. About one out of eleven men will develop prostate cancer during their lifetime, with 80 percent of the cases diagnosed in men over age sixty-five. Prostate cancer is the third leading cause of cancer deaths among men, after skin and lung cancer. Surgery, alone or in combination with radiation and/or hormones and chemotherapy, is the treatment.

Among elderly women, breast cancer is a prime concern. About one in ten women will develop the disease, which killed an estimated 43,000 women in 1989. Women over fifty are at risk, especially if they have a family history of the disease, have never had children, or had their first child after the age of thirty. Treatment includes removal of the breast or the tumor itself, radiation, and chemotherapy.

Lung cancer, the leading cause of cancer deaths, killed more than 140,000 Americans in 1989. Now surpassing breast cancer as the number one cancer killer of women, the incidence of the disease rises sharply after age fifty-five. Among the risk factors are cigarette smoking, exposure to asbestos, and air pollution. Treatment includes surgery either alone or combined with radiation and anticancer drugs. One problem with lung cancer is that it is difficult to detect early because symptoms do not appear until the disease has advanced considerably. People who have been smoking for many years are, of course, most susceptible. Those who quit early, before changes in the cells lining their lungs get out of hand, can usually expect the lining to return to normal.

Again, the longer one lives the better the chances of getting a cancer. People over forty should be encouraged to have a cancer checkup every year, especially if they have been longtime smokers or have been sun worshippers for years (some 500,000 cases of skin cancer caused by excessive exposure to the sun are diagnosed every year in the United States).

Not all cancers can be prevented, but the ones that can — lung and skin, for example, and perhaps colon cancer by eating a high-fiber diet — should have your attention. It has been estimated that by eliminating cigarette smoking alone cancer incidence and mortality would be cut by 15 to 35 percent. You can help the elderly people around you by trying to get them to avoid the environmental hazards that are known to cause some forms of cancer. Practice what you preach, as well. And learn to spot cancer's seven warning signals:

- Change in bowel and bladder habits.
- Any sore that does not heal.
- Unusual bleeding or discharge.
- A thickening or lump in the breast or elsewhere.
- Indigestion or difficulty in swallowing.
- Any obvious change in a wart or mole.
- A nagging cough or hoarseness.

What if an elderly person in your family has cancer?

Obviously, treatment is up to the doctor. But because some forms of treatment — radiation and chemotherapy — may cause unpleasant side effects, the cancer patient needs a good deal of reassurance and support from family members. Patients may become nauseated or lose their hair. Sometimes a cancer patient becomes depressed and feels that it's not worth enduring all the discomfort and pain that might occur and may even want to be left to die. Given that cancer will strike three out of four families, it is not inconceivable that you are or will be part of such a scenario. There are places where you can learn more about how to cope with a family member with cancer. One is the American Cancer Society, which has divisions throughout the United States. Its national headquarters is at 1599 Clifton Road, N.E., Atlanta, Georgia 30329. Another is the National Cancer Institute Office of Cancer Communications, Building 31, Room 10A18, Bethesda, Maryland 20892. The Cancer Information Service has a toll-free number you can call: 800-4-CANCER.

Again, not all of the elderly are destined to have one or more of the diseases we have listed. Some people get to remarkably old ages without having been to a hospital or required to take medication. But age does make a person more vulnerable, and the more you know what *can* happen to an elderly individual, the better you will be able to deal with a health problem should one arise. You might well be the one person who can help keep an elderly parent or grandparent independent longer and, by so doing, reduce the necessity for costly, long-term care.

5 ∎
PROBLEMS WITH LIVING

"No skill or art is needed to grow old; the trick is to endure it."
—Johann Wolfgang von Goethe (1749–1832)

Enduring old age is, indeed, one of the most difficult things the elderly must do. Apart from the physical ailments that afflict many older people, there are behavioral and other mental difficulties to be dealt with. Not that aging inevitably causes mental illness or, for that matter, loss of intelligence. It does not, no more than it causes any of the other diseases and ailments we mentioned in the last chapter. The elderly are, after all, individuals, just as young people are. Each old person is the product of his or her own special biological mold and the environment in which she or he lives and works. Mental illness obviously occurs among the elderly, but more often than not old people who are seriously emotionally unbalanced were probably that way long before they grew old. The complex combination of heredity and environment was most likely responsible for any severe mental instability that may occur, not the process of aging. Even Alzheimer's disease may be inherited because some genetic factor makes some people more susceptible than others.

Unfortunately, many people, among them health professionals who deal with the elderly in nursing homes and other institutions, often fail to understand that many things are behind mental illness in the aged. A report in the journal *American Psychologist* put it this way: "Stereotypic assumptions that normal aging involves a loss of intellectual and emotional competence can conceal the fact that the majority of today's mentally ill aged individuals have grown old with mental illness, not into it."[1] As a result, some doctors and nurses overlook or ignore real psychological problems, attributing them instead to just growing old. Sometimes the health-care people take that stand because they want to avoid demeaning the elderly by diagnosing a mental illness. But whatever the reason — be it an attempt to avoid discriminating against the elderly or the result of lack of understanding of the very nature of mental illness — such a belief often denies treatment to the elderly who may need it, because it carries with it the erroneous notion that psychological problems of the elderly are consequences of the inevitable decline that accompanies aging.

This being said, the other side of the coin is that

although large numbers of the elderly may not be mentally ill — indeed, studies have shown that people sixty-five and older have the lowest overall rates of mental disorders of all age groups — old people are at great risk of having a variety of emotional problems. Sometimes these can be mild bouts of anxiety or sadness, feelings that all of us experience now and then. At other times, the emotional upheaval becomes more serious, resulting in severe depression, alcoholism, perhaps even suicide. The reasons behind an elderly person's emotional ups and downs are many and varied. Often there is a tendency to think more of how few years one has left than, as young people generally do, of how many years have gone by. Beginning typically in one's fifties, people often realize that one is growing old, that a heart attack or cancer might strike, that friends are beginning to die. Older people may become upset when they discover that employers are not as eager to hire them anymore, that they may not be attractive any longer to the opposite sex, or that they may not have enough money to allow them to live the way they would like to live, perhaps the way they used to live when they were younger. Let's examine a few of the emotional troubles the elderly are prone to.

DEPRESSION

All of us, as you well know, have down days, times when we are feeling glum. There are plenty of words for it: unhappy, sad, heavy-hearted, wretched, miserable, discouraged, despondent, blue. In the grip of such down-ers, we may not feel much like eating or carrying on a conversation even with old friends. We may not be able to sleep, so preoccupied are we with what it is that is troubling us. It could be that we have suffered a loss of some sort — a relative or friend, perhaps, a pet, a favor-ite article of clothing or jewelry, a tennis match. We may have flunked an important exam or cracked up the fam-ily car. When we are feeling low because of events like those, we say that we are depressed.

But although the word *depressed* does mean dejected, in the sense that psychiatrists and psychologists use it it can be far more serious than the sadness we feel when things don't go exactly as we wish. This form of depres-sion is common and normal. It usually goes away with time, just as the sun returns after a cloudy day. Even the devastating sadness that we feel after the death of a loved one can be expected to lighten and eventually dis-appear. Such depression is part of the natural grieving process and is temporary. True depression is another matter. It is a complicated illness — or rather, illnesses, since there are so many different types — with many causes. It goes on and on with no letup, and no matter how hard depressed persons try — if indeed they try at all — they cannot free themselves from their dark world. A truly depressed individual has great difficulty making it through a day. He or she may not feel like doing the things that once were delightful or may be unable to perform ordinary tasks like putting out the rubbish. Sleep often not only is impossible but becomes what the person wants to do all day long. A depressed person feels hopeless and helpless, cries without apparent reason, lacks even the trace of a sense of humor, cannot enjoy a happy event, and often loses great amounts of weight due to loss of appetite. Anxiety, the uneasiness of mind that comes with the anticipation of misfortune or danger, is blown all out of proportion to the events that trigger it. Such a person is mentally ill, that is, he or she is sick enough to require professional help. Without help, many depressed people suffer the most serious consequence of their illness: suicide.

The elderly seem to be especially prone to depression: at least 15 percent of those over the age of sixty-five are affected by it to some degree, with women more likely to suffer. Biological, sociological, and psychological factors, many of them associated with aging, may be behind the depression. Put another way, we might say that heredity, disease, and events that occur in one's life are the causes. When someone suffers from a depression because of things that happen to him or her — retirement, widowhood, changes in financial status, the deterioration of physical health, the death of friends — it is referred to as a *reactive* depression. Because older people suffer so many losses — everything from their self-esteem to good health to children who move away — it is no wonder that many of them feel helpless and find their mental stability shaken. "These losses are compounded by the lack of opportunity to compensate for them," said one report on the subject. "Spouses and life-long friends who die are not easily replaced. Older people have fewer resources to draw upon; some lack the social skills to begin anew. Another psychological factor is that some older people view themselves in terms of the negative stereotypes of old age. Believing the myths concerning inevitable, debilitating mental and physical decline can lead to pessimism about abilities and self-worth."[2]

Sometimes the depression comes from within the individual. This is called *endogenous* depression. This condition may be the result of an inherited factor that makes a person susceptible to the disease — some disturbance, deficiency, or overabundance of certain brain chemicals. This does not mean that there is a gene that codes for depression, as there are genes that dictate the color of our eyes or shape of our noses. What does happen, however, is that a person may inherit a *tendency* to develop a mental illness by inheriting a defect in brain chemistry that creates an imbalance of key chemical transmitters.

Another endogenous cause of depression is disease. This is not a case of reactive depression that results when someone finds out she or he has a life-threatening illness but one in which the disease itself causes depression. For example, tumors — among them those of the pancreas — are known to be associated with depression. This seems to be so because tumors may secrete hormones that act on the brain and alter one's mental state.[3] Stroke, a disease that occurs most often among elderly males, can also cause depression, especially when the stroke occurs in the left frontal lobe of the brain. The frontal lobes, left and right, are regions with many functions, among them the regulation of complicated behavior and personality. When the stroke hits this area of the brain, the neurotransmitters that control mood may be damaged.

Another internal cause of depression is associated with the side effects of certain medications, especially when they are combined with other drugs, even those that are bought in a drugstore without a prescription. The elderly are especially vulnerable to experiencing a drug reaction simply because they are more sensitive to many drugs, and because they generally take far more medicines than younger people do. A third of all people over age sixty take five or more drugs at the same time; the average nursing home patient takes seven drugs a day. Among these drugs are tranquilizers to relieve tension, sleeping pills, and antidepressants. While such medicines have their place in treatment, too often they interact with each other and cause a number of adverse reactions, one of which can be a depressed mood. Heightening the risk is the fact that an elderly person's body processes drugs differently. For example, one popular tranquilizer, Valium, clears the body of a young person in twenty-four hours, but takes seventy-five hours to do so in an older person.[4] Thus, drugs can accumulate in an elderly person's body and increase the potential for side effects when they mix. You should also know that older women use drugs at a rate 2.5 times that of older men and are particularly likely to take and overuse so-called psychotropic drugs — drugs that have an effect on brain cells.[5]

This doesn't mean that elderly women inevitably experience more psychological problems than men. They may however, be at greater risk for depression and anxiety since they generally outlive men. Thus they must suffer all of the consequences of widowhood, among them loneliness, stress, the loss of steady income, and, if they do find work, the likelihood that they will not have the same advantages on a job that a man might.

While drugs, either alone or in combination, can be dangerous, they still are a mainstay in the treatment of depression, along with psychotherapy and another treatment we'll discuss later, shock therapy. It is, therefore, important that you know something about the drugs your grandparents may be taking if they are under treatment for depression or other emotional problems. There is a bewildering array of such drugs. Some of the more common ones you may hear about include Valium, Librium, Elavil, Sinequan, Tofranil, Vivactil, Norpramin, Marplan, Nardil, Ritalin, lithium, Haldol, Mellaril, and Thorazine. There are many more, or course, and none are to be taken lightly.

Many antidepressant drugs — they belong to chemical families with complicated names such as heterocyclic antidepressants and monoamine oxidase inhibitors — are powerful enough to restore the brain's normal chemical activity and actually reverse the chemical errors that have created the depression. Others, like tranquilizers, can relieve some of the tension that comes with depression, but do not actually get at the disease itself.

As valuable as they are, however, most of the drugs

can cause adverse side effects. Sometimes the side effects are not too worrisome: constipation, dryness in the mouth, blurred vision. But they can be more serious. Antidepressants, for example, can affect the way the heart and circulatory system work, and some should be used with great care by patients with heart disease or high blood pressure. So-called major tranquilizers, such as Haldol and Thorazine, can give a patient uncontrollable facial twitches. If there is too much lithium in a person's blood, coma or seizures may result. Even the minor tranquilizers, such as Valium, can cause difficulties because they are often abused by the elderly, who may have a tendency to take them indiscriminately whenever they are feeling low. Because of such problems, the doctor who prescribes them for your aging parent or grandparent has to choose each medicine carefully. Each one also has a specific way of acting and may be effective in one person but not so effective in another. Sometimes a patient responds rather quickly to a certain dosage of an antidepressant, other times no improvement is seen for weeks. Sometimes the dosage has to be increased, or the drug must be combined with another. It is not merely a matter of getting a depressed person to a doctor for some medicine.

Another way of treating depression is with electroconvulsive therapy (ECT), popularly known as shock therapy. If you have seen the movie *One Flew Over the Cuckoo's Nest* you know what shock therapy is, but unfortunately the portrayal is not very accurate. The procedure is not painful nor does it leave those who have had it living vegetables. In fact, ECT is a very effective treatment — some say it is the most effective — for carefully selected cases of severe depression in the elderly. Indeed, without shock therapy, many more depressed older people would undoubtedly commit suicide because it usually takes weeks of testing with several antidepressant drugs to find the best one for a particular patient, and weeks more for it to take effect. Also, some patients are so depressed that they forget to take their medicine. Other reasons for using shock therapy are that the side effects are minimal compared with those caused by antidepressants, and that patients generally return to work and a normal life, undazed by drugs, faster. In a survey conducted by the American Psychiatric Association, 92 percent of the psychiatrists who used ECT reported that none of their patients was permanently unable to perform specific jobs after the treatment.[6]

Exactly how shock therapy lifts depression — improvement occurs in a matter of days, not weeks, as with drug treatment — is unclear. It has been suggested that the electric current, applied for a fraction of a second through electrodes held at the side of the head, increases the amount of a key neurotransmitter, called norepinephrine. Deficiency of this brain chemical has been linked to depression. Shock may also boost the activity of another chemical that plays an important role in making norepinephrine.

If your parent or grandparent must undergo shock therapy, forget the brutal scenes involving the horrid Big

Nurse in *Cuckoo's Nest* who relied on shock therapy to keep her patients in line. The treatment, done in a hospital, is far less traumatic than many other procedures, including a stint in a dentist's chair. Before receiving ECT, patients are usually given a tranquilizer or a sedative to relieve anxiety. Then they are put to sleep with a general anesthetic, and while they are asleep the brief pulse of electricity is applied. The electricity causes a form of seizure in which the facial muscles stiffen and the limbs jerk. In the old days of shock therapy, such movements were fairly violent. But today, a drug that acts as a muscle relaxant, administered while the patient is asleep, makes the spasms hardly noticeable. When the patient wakes up, usually he or she is aware of time, place, and date and can talk lucidly. The procedure is generally repeated three times a week for two to four weeks.

There are some side effects that accompany shock therapy. One may be confused just after the treatment and may have a slight memory loss. Most researchers, and the doctors who administer ECT, say that these side effects are mild and temporary and that permanent memory loss is very rare. You should know, however, that many critics of ECT argue that the procedure does have long-term side effects, including permanent loss of some important memories and a decreased ability to retain new information.

Again, the kind of treatment for depression must depend on the patient's doctor and, of course, on the patient. Remember, though, that neither shock therapy nor drugs are cure-alls for depression. Although each has its place you must not forget that social contact, the support of relatives and friends, and professional counseling are also important. It takes more than a pill or a jolt of electricity to keep "the black dog" — as British Prime Minister Winston Churchill called depression — chained. Often, psychotherapy is combined with drugs or ECT in treating depression. One fairly new approach, called reminiscence therapy, encourages the elderly to tell their life stories. By unburdening themselves, their moods often change for the better. Other forms of psychotherapy are aimed at getting the depressed person to increase the number of pleasant experiences during a day. This is based on the notion that everything we do affects our mood — the fewer pleasant things that happen to us, the worse we feel; the more, the merrier, you could say.

No one kind of psychotherapy has all the answers. But all of them share certain characteristics, "Invariably, they seek to promote your parent's sense of self-esteem and self-sufficiency," says psychiatrist David Tomb of the University of Utah School of Medicine. "They explore the impact changing physical health and loss of independence have on your parent. They help your parent wrestle with losses and come to grips with and resolve unsettled feelings about being old. They help your parent establish appropriate, realistic goals. Whatever type of therapy is settled on, most of the gains are made in the first several months; only very unusual circumstances should require treatment past six months or a year."[7]

But it is not always easy to help depressed persons.

Dr. Tomb points out that some of them may not see themselves as depressed, or they may feel so hopelessly depressed that they resist any treatment. "They may insist on being bedridden," he says, "or they may be dependent and demanding, and refuse to participate in self-care in any way. A depressed person may insist that he can't get out of bed, walk, or feed himself. He may feel so completely helpless and hopeless that his only relief is to get you to participate in his misery." Those who deal with such individuals, Dr. Tomb suggests, must avoid playing along with this self-destructive behavior. The caregiver must insist that the patient try to do things for himself or herself.

"Finally," Dr. Tomb says, "don't try to turn your parent's life around all by yourself. Encourage your parent's independence. Utilize groups, organizations, concerned friends, and professionals. Churches, your state's Department of Aging, and public mental health organizations all may offer valuable services."[8]

With the proper help, depressed elderly people can shift gears and live a comfortable life. More than that, they may be saved from taking a fatal step.

SUICIDE

There are times when a seemingly untroubled individual takes his or her own life. We read in the newspapers, for example, of the suicide of a teenager who, according to her neighbors and family, never ever showed any signs of despondency. Her death came as a complete surprise to all who knew her. Or we hear of an ailing, handicapped elderly person taking his life because he can no longer afford to pay for his care and does not want to burden his relatives. A perfectly justifiable, rational act, we might say.

As tempting as it may be to believe that suicide can be committed by someone who is in complete control of his or her senses, generally speaking, as the French writer Voltaire put it, "it is not in an access of reasonableness that people kill themselves." Suicide is a form of murder, probably the worst form, because, as has been said, it does not give the killer time to repent. And when people murder, be it others or themselves, they rarely, if ever, are guided by the accepted, normal rules of society. The taking of a human life is the ultimate flouting of the laws of both government and nature. One never kills without something clouding the difference between right and wrong, between rational and irrational behavior.

When someone is depressed, he or she is not thinking straight. And suicide is quite often part of that skewed thinking. Of course, not all depressed people kill themselves. Many of those who suffer from the various forms of depression can be helped, and their impulse to self-destruct — an impulse that is very often present in cases of depression — can be quieted. Still, an estimated 15 percent of the depressed do kill themselves, as do as many as 25 percent of untreated manic-depressives. (Manic depression is a form of mental illness in which

the patient alternates between periods of high excite-
ment and depression.)[9]

The elderly especially are at risk of suicide. In fact, a
fourth of all suicides in the United States are committed
by people over sixty-five. It was not always so. For many
years, the suicide rate among the elderly declined steadily. But in the 1980s, more and more older people began
killing themselves. According to the latest government
statistics, the suicide rate among those sixty-five and
older is 21.6 per 100,000 people, compared with an overall national rate of 12.8. (The rate for people age fifteen
to twenty-four is around 13.1 per 100,000.)

There are several explanations for the increase, but
depression in one form or another seems to be behind
most of them. Elderly white men, for example, commit
suicide far more often than blacks and women, perhaps
because they generally have been more successful in
their work; when they retire, the shock may be greater
than it might be for someone who has not achieved as
much, and they become unhappy. Retired executives
who have been used to giving orders fall into this category. As one suicide expert put it, "They hate to admit
they have a weakness."[10] This is probably the reason
why so few elderly people who are contemplating suicide seek help: it has been reported that less than 3 percent of the calls to suicide prevention centers come from
people over sixty-five.[11]

Another explanation for the increase in suicide among
the aged has to do with what some call rational suicide.

This occurs when an old person decides that although he or she may live a long life, the quality of that life, because of sickness or lack of money, won't be acceptable. "Medical technology many have created physically longer lives, but it also has created new concerns," psychologist John McIntosh of Indiana University has observed. "People say, 'I'm going to live longer, but is that going to be the kind of life I want to live?'"[12] Dr. Robert Butler, chairman of the Department of Geriatrics at the Mount Sinai School of Medicine in New York City, says, "There's a much greater awareness of Alzheimer's disease and other incurable diseases, and people know they're going to become helpless and the costs are going to be great."[13]

When the elderly begin thinking like that, they may regard suicide as the only way out. According to one report, membership in the Hemlock Society, a right-to-die group that believes people with terminal illness should have the right to take their own lives, has increased to 13,000 members from a relative handful when it was organized in 1980.[14] In Japan, the National Police Agency reported that more people age sixty and older were committing suicide because of illness while the number of non-illness-related suicides among that age group decreased.

Sometimes an old person's grown children contribute to the idea of rational suicide — not deliberately, but by not arguing against the suggestion that the family would be better off without him or her. Sometimes, too, children can push an elderly, troubled parent over the edge by neglecting the little things that mean so much to the parent. A few years ago, a seventy-two-year-old retired accountant with Parkinson's disease became convinced he was becoming a burden to his children. When he didn't receive a card on Father's Day, he swallowed a bottle of sleeping pills. Fortunately, his life was saved. Later, he began a treatment program that combined antidepressant drugs and group therapy. His children moved him to an apartment closer to them and paid more attention to him. Eventually, his spirits lifted.

If your elderly grandparent has attempted suicide — or even mentions it — he or she needs help. There is no way to predict with certainty who will or will not commit suicide, and anyone who threatens to do so must be taken seriously. Insofar as the notion of rational suicide is concerned, we must draw a distinction between allowing a terminally ill person to die with dignity and allowing people to kill themselves because they are a burden to others or because they have simply decided their lives are not worth living. Few doctors and theologians would agree that one must keep a terminally ill patient alive with extraordinary measures. There comes a point in a dying patient's care when he or she must be allowed to decide — either personally to the doctors or in a so-called living will that spells out how much treatment should be given when death nears — whether life is to go on or be stopped. Such a decision, which must often be made by a dying patient's family in cases when the patient is unable to communicate, only hastens the dying. It is not murder when someone makes the decision, and it is not suicide in the true sense of the word when the patient decides to let go. But allowing an elderly person to commit suicide when terminal illness is not an issue is another matter. For one thing, the law does not allow it. For another, whenever someone insists he or she is planning to die, the statement can quite often be taken as a last-ditch plea for help. The elderly parent who tells his or her children they'd be better off with the parent out of the way may only be asking the children to offer some expression of love. Such an offer could save a life.

ALCOHOLISM

Whether alcoholism is a true disease or, as many people believe, a vice, is a question fraught with controversy. Nor can anyone say for sure whether alcoholism is inherited or caused by our environment, whether people drink because they are depressed, or depressed because they drink, whether there is much difference between alcoholism and what we sometimes call problem drinking. It is not my purpose to make any judgments, if only because alcoholism is too complicated a matter, and definitive statements are best left to the experts who, though they rarely agree, can at least offer convincing arguments for one side or the other.

I can say, however, that alcoholism is a disorder that plagues both the young and the old. It is difficult to tell how many users and abusers of alcohol there are, perhaps because so many people drink and because of the various definitions of alcoholism. Billions of gallons of wine, beer, and hard liquor are consumed in the United States every year, and surveys indicate that more than half of all American adults — roughly 100 million people — drink at least occasionally. Out of the total, there may be as many as 10 million people whose drinking has created problems for themselves or their families and friends.

Accurate figures on how many of the elderly have alcohol problems are not easy to come by. For one thing, some of the symptoms of overdrinking in an old person — unsteadiness and confusion, for example — may appear to be the result of age, and relatives and doctors may not consider alcohol the cause. Also, the elderly do not "hang out" in bars as frequently as the young, and are thus able to hide their drinking behavior from others for longer periods of time. Retirement also enables them to drink in private, away from colleagues on the job who might have taken notice of an alcohol problem. Few of the elderly are charged with driving under the influence of liquor, another factor that makes it difficult to document drinking problems. There may be another reason we don't see too many elderly alcoholics around: people who have been drinking heavily for years often do not live long enough to be counted among the elderly.

There seems to be some agreement that alcoholism is less common among the elderly than among young adults. Many people tend to drink less as they grow older, perhaps because they are aware that alcohol "goes to the head" faster with age, or because liquor is too expensive for them. But while there may be fewer older alcoholics than younger ones, the fact is that alcoholism does exist among the elderly, especially among men who overused alcohol in their youth to deal with stressful events in their lives. It has been estimated that one in four hospitalized patients over age sixty — some studies say 60 percent — are or have been dependent on alcohol. Elderly alcoholics are more likely than younger alcoholics to drink every day, and they stay drunk longer because of the increased effect of alcohol on the aged metabolism. Scientists know that after age fifty-five, smaller amounts of alcohol produce high blood levels; thus, if an elderly person has four or five drinks a day — the average that an older alcoholic consumes each day — serious medical problems can arise, problems that are magnified if, as is quite likely, the person takes a number of medications. One of the diseases that alcohol exacerbates is Parkinson's disease.

While some experts maintain that few older persons start drinking heavily in their later years, others claim that a third of elderly alcoholics had no history of alcohol abuse but started drinking late in life because of retirement, loneliness, or financial troubles. Also, between 5 and 15 percent of elderly people with alcohol problems suffer from some form of depression that was there before they began drinking. Alcohol also seems to play a role in about a third of the suicides that occur among the elderly.[15]

How do you tell if your parent or grandparent has a drinking problem? Here are some questions you might ask yourself. The more yes answers you come up with, the more you should be concerned.

- Do you smell alcohol on their breath more frequently than in the past, particularly in the mornings?
- Do they seem to be drinking more when they are depressed, worried, or alone?
- Do they drink much too fast?
- Do they lie about how much they drink?
- Are they falling down and injuring themselves more often?
- Have they actually gotten drunk several times in the past year?
- When they are not drinking, do they appear to become more irritable?

Although alcoholism can be a more devastating disorder in older people, one bright side of the picture is that the elderly usually respond better and more quickly to treatment than the young do. Alcoholics Anonymous has an outstanding record in getting an alcoholic to break the habit, and you should encourage a parent or grandparent with a drinking problem to seek help from organizations like that. Remember that alcohol abuse is bad for any age group. But in the elderly it can be especially dangerous, if only because alcohol affects the brain — and the brain of an older person is already undergoing changes that affect memory, learning, even sleep patterns. Adding alcohol to the detrimental changes that accompany the normal aging process is only adding fuel to the fire.

6 ▪
PUTTING DOWN
THE ELDERLY

"Meanwhile, the sun set, and ... out came an ugly old woman, thin and yellow, with great red eyes, and a crooked nose which reached down to her chin."
— From *Jorinde and Joringel,* by the Brothers Grimm

The fairy-tale character of the old woman who is a wicked witch is a familiar one to all of us. Unfortunately, the caricature is not limited to the fantasy world. We opened this book with some negative stereotypes about old people, written not by fiction writers but by students in your age group. "Crabby," was one characterization. "Smelly breath," was another. And "feeble," "don't understand anything," "body starts to deteriorate," "wrinkly skin," "ready to die."

The young adults who offered those views are not alone, nor can they be blamed for believing them. For hundreds of years, the young, and even the old themselves, have been conditioned to favor youth over age. Sometimes, the aged are objects of ridicule, sometimes of contempt. More often than not, they are pitied. Consider the following from *The Passionate Pilgrim*, a collection of poems published in 1599:

> *Crabbed Age and Youth*
> *Cannot live together;*
> *Youth is full of pleasance,*
> *Age is full of care;*
> *Youth like summer morn,*
> *Age like winter weather;*
> *Youth like summer brave;*
> *Age like winter bare.*
> *Youth is full of sport*
> *Age's breath is short;*
> *Youth is nimble, Age is lame;*
> *Youth is hot and bold,*
> *Age is weak and cold;*
> *Youth is wild, and Age is tame.*
> *Age, I do abhor thee;*
> *Youth, I do adore thee. . . .*

Can you see the similarities in this bit of verse to some of the negative comments the students made? Considering what you have learned in reading this far, which of the lines above, and which of your fellow students' comments, seem unduly harsh?

Now read this excerpt from *As You Like It,* by William Shakespeare:

> *All the world's a stage,*
> *And all the men and women merely players.*
> *They have their exits and their entrances,*
> *And one man in his life plays many parts,*
> *His acts being seven ages. At first the infant,*
> *Mewling and puking in the nurse's arms.*
> *Then the whining schoolboy, with his satchel*
> *And shining morning face, creeping like snail*
> *Unwillingly to school. And then the lover,*
> *Sighing like furnace, with a woeful ballad*
> *Made to his mistress' eyebrow. Then a soldier,*
> *Full of strange oaths and bearded like the pard,*
> *Jealous in honor, sudden and quick in quarrel,*
> *Seeking the bubble Reputation*
> *Even in the cannon's mouth. And then the justice,*
> *In fair round belly with good capon lin'd,*
> *With eyes severe and beard of formal cut,*
> *Full of wise saws and modern instances;*
> *And so he plays his part. The sixth age shifts*
> *Into the lean and slipper'd pantaloon,*
> *With spectacles on nose and pouch on side;*
> *His youthful hose well sav'd, a world too wide*
> *For his shrunk shank; and his big manly voice,*
> *Turning again toward childish treble, pipes*
> *And whistles in his sound. Last scene of all,*
> *That ends this strange eventful history,*
> *Is second childishness, and mere oblivion —*
> *Sans Teeth, sans eyes, sans taste, sans everything.*

The word *sans* in that last line means "without." Does that sum up what aging is all about? Shakespeare was a great poet, but are his observations on aging an accurate portrayal of the process?

Let's look at one more, from Jonathan Swift, the English satirist and poet:

> *Poor gentleman! he droops apace!*
> *You plainly find it in his face.*
> *That old vertigo in his head*
> *Will never leave him till he's dead.*
> *Besides, his memory decays:*
> *He recollects not what he says;*
> *He cannot call his friends to mind:*
> *Forgets the place where he last din'd;*
> *Plyes you with stories o'er and o'er;*
> *He told them fifty times before.*

Even though Swift is talking about one gentleman, does the poem leave the impression that all elderly people are suffering from Alzheimer's disease?

People like Shakespeare and Swift wrote down their negative comments several hundred years ago. But attitudes have not changed much. Jokes about the aged and growing old abound today. Many of them deal with lack of physical strength and mental powers, and about the way one looks. We hear stories about old maids who cannot catch a man, about the dirty old man who is always lusting after a young girl. "My wife hasn't had a birthday in thirty years" is illustrative of the sort of joke that deals with hiding one's age. Comedian Jack Benny was forever thirty-nine. And always, death hovers in the background. "Old age isn't so bad," says one classic one-liner, "when you consider the alternative." Even so successful a writer as W. Somerset Maugham saw fit to moan on his ninetieth birthday: "I am sick of this way of life. The weariness and sadness of old age make it intolerable. I have walked with death in hand, and death's own hand is warmer than my own. I don't wish to live any longer." Grim words to be sure.

The fact remains that age is generally out, youth is in, and it was always so, at least in our society. Not only is the emphasis on being young so pervasive, sometimes it is carried to ludicrous extremes. When Brooke Shields was nineteen, she apparently was concerned about her future. "I'm sure I'll soon be striving to look young," she told an interviewer. "I always used to be the youngest model, and now the hot models are sixteen."[1]

The favored status that youth holds in our society and the uselessness of older people are also notoriously evident in professional sports. Players over thirty are the grandfathers of their leagues, and when they do play sportswriters have to call attention to their age. When Keith Hernandez and Gary Carter, at age thirty-five, didn't have their contracts renewed by the New York Mets because of an emphasis on youth for the 1990s, they were pretty much written off as Golden Agers. "Senior stars," was the way one newspaper columnist kindly referred to them. When Tommy John, at forty-six, was pitching for the New York Yankees in the 1989 season, he was the oldest active player in the majors. Hardly a sportscaster or sportswriter could resist referring to him as a "geriatric case," or "close to Medicare age," or saying that he had been in the game so long it took six pages in the team's information booklet to cover his career. Wrote one writer in the *New York Times* after

John's season-opening start against the Minnesota Twins: "John had his shaky moments, but he pitched well, adding more evidence to the notion that baseball people should not discriminate against senior citizens."[2] When forty-six isn't old enough, one can always lump a couple of players together to come up with something even older. When forty-year-old Jerry Reuss was pitching for the Chicago White Sox, his catcher was forty-one-year-old Carlton Fisk, making them "the oldest battery to team up for an opening-day game in the majors." The writer of that went on to add: "Previously, the oldest opening-day battery was the pitcher Johnny Niggeling and the catcher Rick Ferrell, a combined 79 years old when they played for the Washington Senators in 1944."[3]

Golfer Lee Trevino astonished just about everyone when he shot a five-under-par 67 in the first round of the 1989 Masters tournament to become, at forty-nine, the oldest man ever to lead the field in any round of the match. Much was made of Trevino's age and bad back, but fortunately Trevino himself didn't read too much into those handicaps. "If I get anything out of this round," he said, "it'll be that there's still a spark in the fireplace. All I got to do is throw the right wood on it."[4]

Sometimes the elder statesmen of sports cause discomfort. The case of Don Nygord, fifty-two, the oldest member of the 1988 United States Olympic team, is one that bears mentioning. Nygord was a shooter in the air pistol and free pistol events who won his spot on the team by beating out younger shooters and placing in the top three. But despite the fact that Nygord had scored more points, there were signs of resentment from various officials who felt the team members should be younger. What he told an interviewer about control, concentration, cunning, and maturity has to be heeded by anyone who is arrogant enough to believe that only youth can achieve. "I feel a pistol shooter doesn't mature until he is at least thirty," he said. "I was told by one person that he was tired of seeing old, fat shooters in international competition. It's a matter of self-control. The skills are acquired fairly early. The rest is self-control."[5]

Sports are not the only endeavors that seem to favor youth over age. The workplace is another. Though there is a law against it, age discrimination in business and government is still with us, albeit more subtly. Men and women who have given many productive years to companies are increasingly being coerced into taking "early retirement," a gentle way of telling someone that he or she is unwanted. Sometimes, in the cruelest employer tactic, a dismissal comes just before a person is eligible for pension benefits. A few years ago, a sixty-year-old seamstress unable to find work because of her age told a task force on aging in New York of how she lost her job in the garment industry two years before she would have been eligible for retirement benefits. "I sew because it's something I've liked to do since I was a girl," she said. " I worked for many years. Now I don't feel good about myself."[6]

The need to be productive is heard again and again from the elderly. A Harris survey indicated that 13 percent of unemployed elderly people living alone would work part-time if they had a choice. Said Manhattan Borough President Andrew Stein, who was chairman of the task force: "They want some dignity. They want to make their own way. They don't want to be taken care of. They don't want to be on welfare. They just want to do their jobs."[7] But employment agencies, as they try to place those supposedly over the hill, acknowledge that it is difficult for a forty-year-old, let alone a sixty-year-old, to find work.

Men and women who feel left out because of their age sadly try to make themselves more desirable by getting facelifts and injections of substances that are supposed to restore their lost youth. Wrote Karen DeCrow, former president of the National Organization for Women: "Our culture is intent on taking the lines out of people's faces — surgically, with costly creams and with fear and trembling — when, in fact, the opposite should be the case. As artists know, if there is anything behind a face, that face improves with age. Lines show distinction and character: They show that one has lived, that one may know something."[8]

Employers prefer young workers not because they hate old people; indeed, many managers are the same age as the workers they are shunting aside. But employers usually opt for younger workers because they may not be as prone to illnesses as older ones. Too many elderly workers on a job could cost the company more in the long run. This is so because the costs of health care and the insurance to cover it have become increasingly high. And not only must many employers pay health benefits for workers who are out sick, but salaries are also often continued when workers are ill and unproductive. Also an experienced worker will generally command a higher salary than someone who is just starting out. It makes a sort of economic sense, therefore, to hire a young, inexperienced worker who will work for less money than a well-trained person will. Some employers, unfortunately, have also bought the myth that the elderly are not as sharp mentally, and that a younger worker is more competent and highly motivated. They are comfortable holding on to those erroneous beliefs and fail to grasp the fact that practical knowledge increases with age and experience, that an older worker may have a far deeper attachment to his or her job than a younger person.

Bad as things often are for the elderly in the job market, they could get even worse if science is ever able to extend our healthy and vigorous years beyond what they are now. Given current negative attitudes toward the elderly, there would undoubtedly be far more antagonism aimed at, say, the worker of eighty-five whom science has now made just as productive as someone half that age.

Fortunately, not all employers feel antagonistic toward the elderly, and many have taken steps toward hiring more older workers, and not only for low-level, unskilled jobs. Here is what one policy study of older workers believes should be the attitude of employers:

■ All perceptions of age should be increased by ten years. A fifty-year-old of today should be viewed as the counterpart of a forty-year-old of 1950.

■ In the absence of specific evidence to the contrary, it should be assumed that an older employee can and will remain productive to age seventy. "A healthy fifty-year-old has twenty years of potential career ahead," the study said.

■ Chronological age is an unreliable criterion by which to judge the value of an employee. "Good performance is good performance and bad performance is bad performance whether the worker in question is twenty-five of sixty-five."

■ As far as possible, policies should be age neutral. The older worker should be free to make choices between working or retiring and between working full-time or part-time. The older worker who elects to continue working should have access to career opportunities or options consistent with his or her aspirations, abilities, and potential.[9]

Wise words, those. It is true that many older workers welcome the opportunity to retire, to take it easier after many years of a full-time job. They may now want to explore some new interest, a part-time job, volunteer work, or just a leisure activity. But whether they do or do not want to quit, the point is that it should be their choice, not that of an employer or a law.

It is no wonder that the negative attitudes toward

aging and the aged have had an effect on many elderly people. Even though an older person may feel good about himself or herself, it won't take long, given the generally low impressions about advancing years that are so prevalent, for gloom and uncertainty to set in. If enough people tell old persons that they are not needed because they are "too old," or signal it by paying little heed to old persons' needs and capabilities, then it becomes easy for the elderly to believe it. The following story by a sixty-five-year-old Japanese woman appeared in a Tokyo newspaper a few years ago. It is a striking example of how an elderly person can become saddened and disillusioned when confronted by the negative feelings of younger people:

The youngest of our seven grandchildren is joining a sports camp during the summer vacation. His mother was originally scheduled to participate as an assistant to the instructor but suddenly became unable to do so. When I volunteered to take her place, my grandson said: "You, Grandma? Oh, no!"

When I reacted with strong disappointment, he was nice enough to change his mind and say: "Okay, you can come but you must not share my bungalow." But problems developed after that.

I went to a nearby park with him for a meeting of children and mothers participating in the camp. When I introduced myself to my grandson's group, the boys I was going to take care of said: "Gee, what bad luck." Or, "Can you swim? I can't save you if you drown." Or, "Oh, oh, this is a bad omen."

I began to have second thoughts about participating. Actually, I feel much younger than my age, am very healthy, can ride a bicycle. I like swimming and most of all, I love children. That's why I had thought that children liked me, too. When I go shopping some neighborhood children offer to go with me. Many children greet me with a hearty "Good morning" and smile at me. Has all this been just because they are nice and wanted to make me happy?

While my mind was going over these things, I realized that children were not the only people I would be dealing with. Other young mothers would find it a burden if an old woman were among the group. If I were to cause unpleasantness by my participation, it would spoil the otherwise very happy camp.

Realizing that I was about to commit a blunder, I offered to quit with apologies to the camp organizers. When I told my husband of my decision, he snapped: "You should have known that before."[10]

Was the woman right in quitting? What do you think of the attitudes of the kids in camp? Do you think the elderly woman's fear about the young mothers was valid? And what of her husband's comment? How do you think he may have been treated by younger people in the past?

There is something else about that story, something that may seem to contradict what we will say later about Asians being more attentive and respectful of the elderly. It is true that the Japanese and Chinese are noted for the way they care for and view the aged. And it is still true that the Japanese, more than Westerners, prefer that the elderly live with their children. There is much we can learn from how Asians generally still treat their old folk.

But times are changing, especially in Japan, which has become one of the world's foremost economic powers and one of the wealthiest. Increasingly, Japan's younger people have grown more self-centered — a trait that has, unfortunately, been all too prevalent in the United States and has drawn criticism from countries like Japan. Individualism has begun to replace the group mentality that has long dominated Japanese society. With the new emphasis on being independent has come a devaluation of tradition. Young people do not want to live in the crowded apartment buildings as their parents did without complaining, even though it meant that three generations lived in the same place. More and more women are seeking careers and equality with men, and many refuse to play nurses to elderly in-laws. Life must go forward, of course, or there would be no intellectual growth, no economic and political strength. But change is not always easy or desirable, and, unfortunately, people often get hurt in the process.

One noted Japanese economist summed up the current situation this way: "With the rapid changes in the nation's economy and society in recent years, the friction resulting from different generations living under the same roof — the old people clinging to the traditional lifestyle and the young people being influenced by newer, Western ways — has become increasingly irksome. Changes in the industrial and employment structures have also made it increasingly difficult for parents and children to live together. In 1960 the proportion of the elderly (aged sixty-five and over) living with their children or other relatives was 87 percent, far higher than in other advanced nations. By 1970, however, this figure had dropped to 76 percent, and since then it has continued to decline."[11] Today, only 45 percent of elderly Japanese live with their children, and in Tokyo, where most families share very cramped quarters, the figure is around 40 percent.

It is not my intention to try to resolve the debate over whether the elderly who cannot care for themselves should live at home or be in a nursing home. Today in the United States 4 to 5 percent of people over sixty-five are in nursing homes, and 20 to 25 percent of the population will eventually spend some time in one. There is widespread disagreement over whether home or nursing home care is better. The answer is often purely personal and dependent on the circumstances of the case. As for the elderly themselves, some say they prefer to live at home, other say no, they do not want to be a burden. If you are ever required to decide how best to take care of elderly parents — and chances are that will happen because your parents probably will live longer then their parents did — your decision must be well thought out. You must carefully weigh the needs, desires, and well-being of your parents and balance them against how much of a burden, financial and emotional, the choice will place on you. Will you be able to afford a nursing home charge? If you cannot, who is going to pay for such care if you decide you are not capable of dealing with an elderly parent with, say, Alzheimer's disease?

These are not easy decisions, nor are there simple answers to such questions. There are, however, things a young person can do to make an elderly person's life easier. It seems obvious that younger people should avoid calling too much attention to an older person's age, especially the sort of attention that buttresses the stereotypes or treats a senior citizen like a child without a mind of his or her own. Your grandparents, after all, have been around for a while. They have had experiences that you have not yet had. They have memories, a whole storehouse of them. They have had hard times and good times, disappointments and victories, many of them linked to rearing and caring for your parents when *they* were children. Most important, they have had to make decisions. That you cannot forget, for it is proof that no matter how irritable they get on occasion, no matter how seemingly inept, they were quite capable individuals. Many of them still are, and they usually know what is best for them. Older is *not* dumber.

You may decide to become a doctor, nurse, or other member of the geriatric health-care team, or a politician. For too long, segments of the medical profession and many public officials who write laws that dictate how the elderly are to be treated have regarded older people as second-class citizens. Most long-term things — such as nursing home care, home health care, home meals, and physical therapy — are not covered by Medicare or private health insurance. This means that the elderly with chronic illnesses, including those with Alzheimer's disease who cannot perform routine daily activities, have to pay for services themselves or go without.

In California, a state where more than 1.1 million people need long-term care because of disabilities and chronic illnesses, the cost of that care is an ever-present problem. According to a 1989 report by researchers at the University of California at San Francisco, the number will grow to nearly 1.6 million in the year 2000 and double to 2.2 million in 2020. "As the demand for services increases, the need for financing mechanisms to cover them becomes a major public policy concern," said Dr. Carroll Estes, who headed the study. "Since the costs of long-term services can often be over $20,000 a year, many individuals, particularly the elderly who have low incomes, become impoverished within a few weeks of the onset of serious disability."[12]

Doctors also have been negligent in caring for the elderly. Many of them have had little training or interest in geriatrics. Many believe that using special technology on an elderly patient is not justified, that such treatment is a waste of scarce and expensive resources best employed on a younger patient who is more likely to survive. But is a person's age the best measure of who should be given special treatment? Should not that decision be based on the person's general health? Can a doctor — or anyone else, for that matter — really do "too much" for an elderly patient?

Too often society continues to make meaningless generalizations about older people. Again, every person, old or young, is an individual, and those individual differences are, according to the experts, greater among the elderly than within any other age group. The American Medical Association's Program on Aging has noted this, and points out that successful living demands that both the elderly and others in society recognize it:

"These differences relate to health, economic condition, social status, education, experience and all of the other factors which set individuals apart. After 60, 70, or 80 years, the sheer number of choices a person has made tends to make him or her vastly different from others."[13]

In discussing how an older person can get the most out of life, the AMA lists six basic considerations that are not only important for the elderly to read, but for you as well since you will be old yourself someday.

1. Meaningful, regular work is important. The job may be a paying one or not, full-time or part-time; anything, so long as it is rewarding in some way.

2. Participation in family activities is something that most seniors are eager to do. On this point, the AMA observes: "Both younger family members and the older persons themselves must work at getting along and be willing to consider modification of their own attitudes toward each other. Family life seems to have an inherent quality of stress built into it. This is true whether all live under one roof, or whether the family is extended over

two or more communities. There are stresses between brothers and sisters, members of the same generation, and between members of different generations. Young and old alike must recognize that stresses are not caused solely by differences in age. Older people must recognize that younger people have many misconceptions about their elders, and not get too upset about it. If at all possible, the older person should make some economic contribution to the family and help with household chores, such as baby-sitting and housework. The key to different generations getting along in the same family is flexibility. The older person must be willing to bend now and then on his demands of the younger person." Let me add that young people, too, must be willing to bend a little when they feel the urge to let an older person know that they are better able to make a decision than he or she is.

3. Another way some people can avoid being characterized as "getting old" is to pay attention to the way they dress and look. If the elders in your family have neglected their appearance, perhaps you can convince them to add some bright clothing to their wardrobe, or to pay more attention to hairstyle and skin care.

4. Recreational activities are essential for the elderly. Recreation doesn't have to be physical, either. Card playing may be chosen because it is competitive, or an older person can go to plays, movies, and spectator sports, with a relative or a friend.

5. The person who lives a full life, regardless of age, is the one who has interest in a great variety of activities

and people. "The person emerging from childhood to adulthood must adopt and accept new responsibilities," says the AMA. "So, too, adults who are in transit to senior citizen status must look for new and wider horizons. If they do not, their attention to, and interest in, the family may pall and its purpose be defeated."

6. Finally, all old people must make a continuous and intelligent appraisal of themselves and their activities. "Successful living calls for such an inventory from time to time by persons of all ages. Perhaps because of the increased tendency of older persons to underestimate their abilities, it is most important for senior citizens to look carefully at themselves and their activities."

If you can get the older people in your life to follow these recommendations, you will be helping them a lot. And because they will be living better lives, adjusting better to their advanced years, any negative feelings you may have about the elderly are almost sure to disappear, and you will get along better with them. One more bit of advice: rather than deny the elderly the respect and the benefits that are due long years of experience, acknowledge old people's status both through your attitudes and your actions. You owe them that, not just because they are older than you, but simply because it is right. Don't take too literally what the Romanian sculptor Constantin Brancusi once said: "When we are no longer young, we are already dead." Instead, maybe the words of Pope John XXIII have a lot more to offer: "Men are like wine — some turn to vinegar, but the best improve with age."

7 ▪

HOW OTHER CULTURES VIEW OLD AGE

"You shall rise before the aged and show deference to the old."
— Leviticus 19:32

Just as we find wicked old witches in fairy tales, myths, and legends, so do we find old people of great powers and wisdom. Job in the Bible is one example. He was already an old man when God tested his faith and endurance by depriving him of his health, his property, and his friends. His faith unshaken, Job survived the ordeal and, when it was over, lived another hundred and forty years. Such an accomplishment earned Job a place among the patriarchs, the wise old men of scripture, and made his name synonymous with extreme patience. Solomon, a son of David and tenth-century B.C. king of Israel, is said to have written the books of Proverbs and

Ecclesiastes when he was well along in years. Proteus, son of Poseidon, Greek god of the sea, was called the Old Man of the Sea and possessed the gift of prophecy. Merlin, a wise man and sorcerer who appears in the legends of King Arthur, is generally depicted as old, with a flowing white beard. The Aleuts of Alaska credit someone called the Old Man with creating people by tossing stones over his shoulder. American Indian tales, too, are filled with references to the notion that old age and wisdom go hand in hand. There is the Old Woman Adviser, who turns up in many so-called test and hero tales. She is a source of guidance and inspiration, advising heroes how to escape traps, kill monsters, select the correct fork in a road, and overcome obstacles. And Old John, the clever slave in the Brer Rabbit stories, matches wits with Old Massa and generally triumphs. Even the animals have their sages. Old Man Coyote of Crow Indian legend is a creator-god and a magician. And of course, there is the bespectacled wise old owl in the equally old oak tree.

From the jolly, bearded, white-haired Santa Claus, who is somehow able to fly over rooftops aboard a reindeer-sleigh and visit homes throughout the world all in a single night, to the delightful, outrageous Wizard of Oz, who allegedly could dispense brains, hearts, and courage as easily as though these things were items on a supermarket shelf, age has often been equated with uncanny powers. Emphasis on the miracles that can be wrought by the elderly is, of course, not always well placed. One can easily find young people who are far wiser than old people and oldsters who are willing to admit it. When, for example, the young man in Lewis Carroll's celebrated nonsense poem, "You Are Old, Father William," questions whether it was right for old Father William to be incessantly standing on his white-haired head, the old man admits that in his youth he feared the practice might injure his brain. "But now that I'm perfectly sure I have none," said Father William, "why, I do it again and again." There is also the character of Old Fortunatus in a play by the sixteenth-century English dramatist Thomas Dekker. An elderly beggar, Fortunatus was offered wisdom, strength, beauty, long life, or wealth by the goddess of fortune. Fortunatus unwisely chose riches, and though he gained a bottomless purse he also was plagued by innumerable troubles until he died miserably.

Still, despite Father William and Old Fortunatus, there is no question that age and experience often win out over youth and inexperience. While the elderly may not have supernatural powers, the very fact that they have been there before — that is, have faced circumstances that they either dealt properly with or learned enough after failing to deal with them to enable them to avoid the same mistake again — gives them a decided advantage over the novice when solving problems on the job, at home, or in relationships with other people. The Roman statesman and orator Cicero (106–43 B.C.) tells us: "It is not by muscle, speed, or physical dexterity that great things are achieved, but by reflection, force of character, and judgment; in these qualities, old age is usually not only not poorer, but is even richer."

Unfortunately, not everyone sees it that way, especially in the Western world. All too often, the old are respected only if their minds are keen as razors. If they are sick and unable to contribute, all of their stored-up knowledge and experience are not worth much. It was not unusual, for instance, for members of some cultures — American Indians among them — to take their unproductive elderly into the desert or up into the mountains and leave them there to die. Some tribes got rid of their elders more quickly. Among the Ojibway of Michigan, the son was selected to do his father in with a tomahawk after first feasting with him, smoking a peace pipe, and singing a death song. In Labrador, a wandering tribe known as the Montagnais used to dispose of the elderly by shooting them with bullets cast from melted-down lead crucifixes given them by missionaries.

Thankfully, such barbaric practices have disappeared, and, indeed, many cultures have developed caring attitudes toward the elderly that we can all learn from. Consider, for instance, the Abkhasians, an apparently very long-lived folk who live in the Caucasus region in the southern Soviet Union. Many Abkhasians, according to some scientists who have studied them, seem to have no trouble living to well over a hundred years old. Advanced age is not viewed, either by themselves or by the younger people around them, as a cloak of infirmity, prescribed and regulated. There is little room for competition, excessive ambition, or any change from the traditional ways. Children may not even talk to parents if their grandparents or other senior relatives are present; in this way, the existence of older persons demands constant attention and respect."[1] The oldest of the Abkhasians are members of a council of elders that not only handles hospitality arrangements for the village, but is regularly approached for advice by the young.

Among the other notable cultures that have learned to respect age as a reward and not a sentence to a dull and shut-in life are the Chinese and Japanese. This is not to say that Asia will always be a haven for the elderly. As we saw, changes in the region's economy and society, along with a rapidly increasing number of older people, are already having a negative effect on the traditional view of aging, an effect that could, sadly, force Asians to take on some of the less desirable attitudes of the Western world toward the elderly. Still, it is well to remember that China and Japan, along with most other Asian countries, have a long history of family structure, religion, attitudes toward retirement, and even literature, that honor old age and give the elderly a respected role in society. The belief is still widespread that old people's past experience makes them valuable to the younger generation. The respect, moreover, is no recent happening. More than four thousand years ago, Huang Ti, the Yellow Emperor (2697–2597 B.C.), wrote: "Those who search beyond the natural limits will retain good learning and clear vision, their bodies will remain light and a mark of feebleness of mind and body, a stage in life when one simply waits out one's time. Abkhasians recognize, instead, that old age is an accomplishment rather than a penalty and as such deserves respect and dignity and, for those who reach it, the opportunity to work productively and live as happily as possible.

Stories about the remarkable activities of Abkhasians abound. There was, for example, Shirali Muslimov, who died in 1973 at the reported age of 168. He worked as a watchman and handyman until his death, riding a donkey over more than five miles of mountain slopes to his job on a farm. Muslimov fathered his last child at the age of 130 and, said his doctors, had the blood pressure of a man in his thirties. Many of the centenarians of Abkhazia seem to have a similar history. Each of those interviewed by scientists were able to care for themselves, could think clearly, and kept up an interest in family and village life. Moreover, as psychologist David Barash of the University of Washington points out, Abkhasians are never made to feel useless. "Significantly," he observes, "they have no word for 'old people.' Rather, they speak of 'long-living' people. The difference is subtle but important; in the Abkhasian phrase 'long-living,' the emphasis is shifted to something positive. Age is seen as an accomplishment that others respect. It is a source of pride. . . . The most important possessions to an Abkhasian are his personal relationships with others: his family, friends, villagers, and visitors. In the rigid, authoritarian Abkhasian system, no counterculture is tolerated, and everything is carefully strong, and although they grow old in years they will remain able-bodied and flourishing, and those who are able-bodied can govern to great advantage." An ancient Chinese poet proclaimed: "Between thirty and forty, one is distracted by the Five Lusts. I have put behind me love and greed. I have done with profit and fame. Still my heart has spirit enough to listen to flutes and strings. At leisure, I open new wine and taste several cups."

Traditionally, Chinese culture has regarded the family as the main provider for the elderly. Most of the credit for such a view goes to one man, Confucius (551–479 B.C.), China's greatest philosopher and sage, who, by the time he died at age seventy-two, had taught more than three thousand disciples who carried on his work. The teachings of Confucius had nothing to do with a supernatural God, as Christianity does. Instead, three major doctrines molded the Chinese character, made it what scholars call "Confucian." The first was benevolence (or humanity), or, in Chinese, *jen*. *Jen* was the quality that distinguished humans from the animals. It was to be cultivated by people within themselves, and the best way to do this, according to Confucius, was to put one's self into the skin of others and then treat them accordingly. Two well-known sayings of Confucius, his Golden Rules, best express the idea of *jen:* "Do not do to others what you would not like yourself," and "Do unto others what you wish to be done unto yourself." As Confucius himself defined it, *"Jen* is to love men." The second Confucian doctrine dealt with the "superior" man, that is, the person who practices benevolence no matter how poor or how rich he or she may be. The third doctrine was called ritual propriety. This referred to all of the correct social behavior that governs the relationship of one person to another. Confucius also stressed the importance of expressing *jen* in the family, for the family was, for him, where all of the doctrines were put to work. A Confucian family was highly structured. The members had to obey the oldest man, wives had to obey their husbands, the son had to obey the father, and the youngest son had to obey his eldest brother.

Contrast that with American families, who are often split into different households, preventing the older generation from sharing in the problems and successes of the younger members of the family. Thus, the American parent who ages may suddenly be transformed from a needed parent to an outgrown one. In many such cases, the elderly end up in nursing homes. The Chinese way, to this day, is to have the children or other family provide food, shelter, clothing, and money to the elderly. There is none of the prejudice noted earlier, ageism, which patronizes and tolerates the elderly in America and treats them like children who are to be seen and not heard. Admittedly, part of the motivation is out of necessity: while such things as retirement plans and old-age pensions are available in some prosperous rural areas — where some 82 percent of China's total elderly population lives — the money an old person can receive varies with the local economic conditions, and is quite often incredibly small by our standards. This means that old people have to depend on their children for most support.[2] But even though there may be no alternative, the fact remains that the children *do* take up the slack, and more often than not they do so without question, aware that not only financial support but love and concern — two essential ingredients that no social institution will ever be able to provide and that only the family can — are essential to the well-being of the elderly. And so, if elderly widows and widowers can find even remote relatives or neighbors to help them, they opt for that rather than live a collective, impersonal life in an old people's home. Even in the relatively few instances when married children live apart from their mothers and fathers the closeness of family is evident. Young husbands and wives often come back to visit their parents to help them manage their affairs, support them financially, share holidays, and accompany them to festivals and neighborhood functions. The bond of family in China can even be close among those who are not related by blood, and it is not uncommon for an aged widow or widower to be living with adopted sons and daughters and in-laws.

Confucianism also emphasizes the importance of ancestors and has a good deal to do with how growing old is regarded in China. Some years ago, two doctors conducted a study in Boston's Chinese community that dealt in part with the impact of Asian religion on successful aging. They explained: "Confucianism is the worship of one's ancestors by honoring them through improving the condition of the family and maintaining its patterns and its unity. The aged are a family's closest connection with its ancestors. Thus, the closer one comes to death, the more honored is one's role. For example, presentation of a coffin or burial clothing, called 'longevity robes,' to one's aged parents is considered an act of filial piety."[3] By contrast, other religions honor just one God and emphasize the individual; they encourage us to rely on ourselves and, generally, to be independent of family and parents. "God helps those who help themselves," is another familiar way of putting it. Or, as one Notre Dame football coach once explained the many successes of his teams, "Prayer helps if the players are big." Such attitudes have undoubtedly helped shape generations of Americans who admire progress — progress usually associated with computer-sharpened, youthful minds.

Interestingly, the Boston study found that most of the Chinese were reluctant to be interviewed, just the opposite of the case among elderly non-Asians in a nearby housing project. Not only were the non-Asians more receptive, but they tended to boast more about their past — perhaps because they felt that their better days were gone, and that the only way they could feel pride was to look backward. The Chinese, on the other hand, had no need to look to past glories, presumably because they had learned to accept old age as a time to enjoy the fruits of a difficult, earlier life. The doctors who conducted the study concluded: "Most Americans feel emptiness if they lack a hobby started before retirement, because they miss a fast-tempo life in a mechanized age. The Chinese does not feel the necessity of taking up time every minute. If he is a peasant, he welcomes the chance to sit back and relax when forced to retire because he has worked hard every minute of his life. If he is a member of the gentry, he probably had leisure all his life, so free time is nothing new to him on retirement."[4]

The Japanese, too, have had a long-standing high regard for the elderly. Although customs are breaking down, the elderly have traditionally relied on their children or in-laws for support, either living with them or nearby. In 1960, some 87 percent of people over sixty-five were living with their adult children and although the number has dropped to around 70 percent, it is still far higher than in the United States, where only about 20 percent of the elderly live with their children. Because so many of the elderly are with their families — and many of the "children" who care for the elderly are themselves in their sixties and seventies — there are far fewer nursing homes in Japan than in the United States. In 1984, it was estimated that there were only 70,000 nursing home beds in the entire country of some 117 million people; the United States, with more than twice that population, has a dozen times as many such beds. Many of the Japanese elderly are bedridden or suffer from the various mental and physical symptoms of senility, but still they are cared for at home. Here, Confucian ways of life are practiced every day and not observed just once a week at a church service, as often is the case in the United States.

Again, Confucian teachings can take much of the

credit. As one Japanese proverb cautions, "When we wish to be dutiful to our parents, they are no more."

Even though they are often cared for by their children, Japanese elders are not generally idle people. While most companies in Japan require workers to retire between ages fifty-five and sixty — in the United States and Europe, sixty-five is generally viewed as retirement age — this does not mean that retirees quit altogether. Close to 80 percent of employees who left their jobs because of their age find other jobs. (In the United States, only about 11 percent of the elderly are employed.) Many Japanese go back to work at their old companies — although often at poorer wages — while others join smaller businesses. Temporary employment agencies, known as Silver Manpower Centers, are scattered throughout Japan, and though the part-time work they offer senior citizens — groundskeeping, balancing a company's books, repairing broken appliances — may not be all that exciting, it does make the workers feel they are still of some value, and it helps offset the enormous cost of caring for an increasingly aging population.

There is an interesting parallel here with another work-oriented society, that of the ancient Incas. The Incas were a highly developed South American Indian people who ruled a vast area that included what we now know as Peru, Bolivia, Colombia, Chile, and Ecuador. From about 1438 to 1532, when they were conquered by the Spanish, the Incas forged a remarkable civilization, digging for gold, building networks of highways, and stringing rope suspension bridges across rivers. They built dams and reservoirs, terraced mountain slopes to grow a wide variety of vegetables, and domesticated animals, notably the llama and alpaca. The Incas were also equal opportunity employers. Simone de Beauvoir, one of France's leading woman writers and author of what is considered the definitive study of the universal problem of growing old, *The Coming of Age*, tells us that from the age of five on, everyone in Incan society was required to make himself or herself useful. The men and women were divided into ten classes each, nine of which were age categories; the tenth comprised those who were sick, crippled, or unable to look after themselves. Each class had its own duties, and was obliged to serve the community to the best of its ability. "Age did not do away with the obligation to work," Madame de Beauvoir writes.

> After they were fifty, the men were exempt from military service and all very laborious tasks, but they had to work in the chief's house and in the fields. They retained their authority within the family. The women over fifty wove cloth for the community or took service in rich women's houses as caretakers and cooks. From eighty onwards the men were deaf and hardly able to do more than eat and sleep; but for all that they were made to be useful. They made ropes and carpets, looked after houses, raised rabbits and ducks, picked up leaves and straw; the old women wove and span, looked after houses, helped bring up children and went on working for the rich, supervising the young servant-

girls. If they had fields of their own they lacked for nothing; if they did not, they were given alms. The men, too: they received food and clothing and their goats were looked after; if they were ill, they were taken care of. Generally speaking, elderly men were feared, honoured and obeyed. They could give advice, instruction and a good example; they could extol right conduct and help in the service of the god. They guarded the younger married women. They had the right to beat unruly boys and girls.[5]

The Incas have disappeared as an empire, but the way they treated the elderly members of their community should not be forgotten. Nor should the teachings of Confucius. They, too, are still valid today as models for how we should treat our own elderly. As you meet old people, as you interact with them in your families, ask yourself some questions. Would you like to be put down because you can't see or hear very well? Is it proper for you to grow impatient with them because they do not move as quickly as you, or listen to the same music as you do? How would you like to be treated if you were in their place? How can you make them feel useful? How can you best show your love for them? If you can't ask such questions and then act in the best interests of the elderly in your life, the chances are they will become truly old.

8 ■
DISPELLING SOME MYTHS OF AGING

"There is a wicked inclination in most people to suppose an old man decayed in his intellects. If a young or middle-aged man, when leaving a company, does not recollect where he laid his hat, it is nothing; but if the same inattention is discovered in an old man, people will shrug up their shoulders and say, 'His memory is going.'"
—Samuel Johnson (1709–1784)

In the preceding chapters you learned about the physical and behavioral difficulties that beset the elderly, and you read some examples of how old people are sometimes ridiculed. Advanced age is not, we know, always a joyous time. The health and emotional problems that face the elderly are very real ones, as we have seen. Even some of the jokes about old people, cruel as they may be, may have a grain of truth in them.

But though the old may be prone to physical and mental decline, that does not mean every old person is confined to a wheelchair or an institution. We know that is not the case. Not all old people sit around and do nothing but watch soap operas on television, play checkers, make birdhouses, or paint by number. Quite often, such simple pastimes are the only pleasures an old person has, and they can help make life worth living for many people. But to believe that old people and hobbies are what old age is all about is a stereotype that should be put to rest. Hobbies are activities *outside* of one's usual occupation, and they are generally engaged in for relaxation. Since many old people are retired, hobbies become quite important. But they are not substitutes for meaningful work and they are not the only activities that old people are capable of. Because so many of the elderly these days are healthier and live longer, many of them, including the so-called old-old, are incredibly active, creative, curious, productive, and enthusiastic. They can write elegant and critically acclaimed books, paint masterful pictures, compose and perform music, act on the stage and in the movies, run in marathons, and learn to fly planes. They govern, travel, enter college, and, yes, fall in love and have sex.

The world is full of old people who have accomplished much in spite of — perhaps even because of — their advanced age. Giuseppe Verdi, the Italian composer, wrote his monumental opera *Falstaff* when he was eighty. Galileo was making discoveries about the movements of the moon when he was in his seventies. Justice Oliver Wendell Holmes was almost ninety-one when he left the U.S. Supreme Court, and architect Frank Lloyd Wright was designing and building impressive structures when he was well into his nineties. Dr.

Jonas Salk, the scientist who developed the first polio vaccine more than three decades ago, was trying to find an AIDS vaccine at the age of seventy-three in 1988. Ronald Reagan was sixty-nine when he was first elected President, and almost seventy-four when he began his second term. Comedians George Burns, age ninety-four at this writing, and Bob Hope, eighty-seven, are still telling jokes on stage, and Hope plays golf as well. Representative Claude Pepper of Florida was the oldest living member of the U.S. Congress when he died in 1989 at the age of eighty-eight. One of his most important accomplishments was a 1986 law that barred mandatory retirement because of age. He said at the time: "Abolishing age discrimination will offer new hope to older workers who are desperate to maintain their independence and dignity."[1] The "grand old lady of American art," Anna Mary Robertson, better known as Grandma Moses, was still painting at 100, the Spanish painter and sculptor Pablo Picasso in his nineties. Indeed artists, generally, seem to manage to go on and on. "Artists do not retire," one critic has observed. " They go on painting, sculpting, drawing, and designing until the last minute, their self-expression too powerful and too hard-won a stimulant to renounce at an arbitrary sixty-fifth or seventieth year. Indeed, the concept of 'retirement' is such a rare and alien thing that when an artist voluntarily stops working . . . the event is noteworthy enough to cause elaborate theories and justifications to be advanced."[2]

The not-so-famous, too, have their elderly stars, people who have done some remarkable things. Helene Schaefer, a great-grandmother from Westchester, New York, got her master's degree in 1989 from Manhattanville College at the age of eighty-nine. In 1981, Teiichi Igarashi, ninety-six, became the oldest man to climb Japan's Mount Fuji. (The previous record was held by a man of ninety-five). There were Wang Ching-chang, ninety-four, of Taiwan, and Herbert Kirk, ninety, of Bozeman, Montana, racing against each other down the home stretch in the 200-meter dash during the 1989 VIII World Veterans Championships. (Wang won by a foot, 52.21 to 52.23.) And Ella Galbraith Miller, the Tennessee-born daughter of freed slaves, at the age of 108 was still going strong. One woman who knew her told this story about the centenarian: "She's a true phenomenon and a constant inspiration. A few weeks ago my thirteen-year-old daughter and some of her friends went over to visit after school. When Mrs. Miller asked if they'd like some ice cream the girls said they would, expecting her to get some from the freezer." Instead, Mrs. Miller lead the way to an ice cream parlor more than two miles away. "Mamma," the visiting teenager said, "Mrs. Miller may walk with a cane, but she's a real speed-demon. We couldn't keep up with her."[3]

It is true, of course, that many people lose their physical energy and mental skills as they age. Alzheimer's disease certainly causes such losses. But more often than not, the elderly are capable of much more than the young realize. So long as they have been spared a serious disease, our old people can function nearly as well as you. When they are not achieving much, they are really not much different from what you would be like if you lived alone, had lost your family and friends, didn't work or study or read or go out. You'd behave a lot like some of the elderly and probably would mope about the house, bury yourself in a hobby, or watch reruns of old movies on television.

There is an old expression, "Use it or lose it." Or as Hippocrates, the ancient Greek physician known as "The Father or Medicine," put it: "Use strengthens, disuse debilitates." This applies both to one's mind and muscles, and to young and old alike. After all, our bodies are like cars and other machines in that they work better when they are tuned. In the case of the elderly, it appears that the physical and mental losses that often accompany aging do not always result from disease or the aging process: quite often these losses are due to the disuse of body and mind. Moreover, it has been shown time and again that when the elderly exercise regularly, and when they are enrolled in educational programs tailored to their needs, their physical and mental deficits are generally erased.

You are all familiar with exercise, the kind you do in gyms and on playing fields and courts. Unfortunately, many of you may be somewhat bemused when you hear of a grandfather or grandmother lifting weights, running on a treadmill, or playing touch football or tennis. Perhaps you feel that they ought to take it easy because they might get a heart attack. Such strenuous activities are best left to the young, aren't they? Well, maybe a little golf is okay for a senior citizen. But shouldn't those old dudes always drive around the course in a golf cart, or employ a caddy? Wrong if you answered yes!

As someone once said, we each have two doctors, our left leg and our right leg, and that goes for both young and old. Brisk walking is, of course, one the best, cheapest, and most pleasant ways to exercise for all of us. For the elderly, it is also the safest since it does not involve the stress on their knees and lower back that comes, for example, with jogging. Doctors say that regular walks are the best way for an elderly person to condition his or her cardiovascular system and ward off or improve osteoporosis, the bone disease we discussed earlier. Moreover, it is an activity that elderly people can participate in without worrying about working up too much of a sweat or without having to gasp for breath when they're trying to have a conversation.

The benefits of walking, even running, for the elderly have been documented by a number of scientific studies. One of these was conducted recently by researchers at the Center on Aging at the University of Maryland, and at the University of Arizona. The study involved forty-five active and inactive men divided among two groups. One group was twenty to thirty years old, the other sixty-one to sixty-nine. The active men had exercised for an average of ten years, running about thirty-seven miles a week. During the test, the men exercised, either by walking or running, on a treadmill for one hour, after which their blood was tested to see how exercise affected their hormone level and their bodies' response to exertion. The results were interesting. While the experiment confirmed that men lose some of their ability to function as they age, the inactive men had the greater loss of function, regardless of age. In general, the older, active men in the study retained their health and were able to do more work — that is, run faster and farther — and with less stress on their bodies' metabolic system, the system that provides energy to our bodies, than the inactive men who were forty years younger. The experiment also supported the conclusion of other studies that long-term exercise prevents the age-associated development of Type II diabetes. (Exercise, it has long been known, burns up excess sugar.) The study concluded: "In terms of having the metabolic wherewithal to provide energy, older runners' bodies are more like young athletes' than they are like the bodies of the old or young sedentary men."[4] That finding was similar to one that emerged several years ago in a study of Finnish long-distance runners as old as seventy-nine. The scientists found that the runners had "younger" heart-lung systems than a group of shopkeepers.

In another study, this one conducted by the U.S. Department of Agriculture Human Nutrition Research Center on Aging at Tufts University, researchers came up with something else that might change the way you feel about old people. They found out that one is never too old to pump iron. The study put a number of men ages sixty to seventy-two through weight-training exercises and eventually got them to improve the size and strength of their muscles. Generally, the men were able to lift weights 80 percent heavier than what they had been able to handle in the past, with one man tripling the strength of his muscles. Said Dr. William Evans, who conducted the study: "Don't have low expectations of older people. Many people believe that the elderly's muscles inevitably atrophy [waste away], but we found that the thigh muscles increased about 11 percent with the weight-lifting. The results show that the elderly can respond just as well as younger people to intensive muscle training. Up until now, we have believed that older people could not do this kind of activity, and therefore we didn't challenge them. Consequently, they didn't see much gain or the point of exercising."

The advantages of such a weight-lifting program for an elderly person are, of course, enormous. Along with the general improvement in health that can result — muscles are also a reservoir of protein, vital for the body to cope with periods of stress such as injury or surgery — exercise helps to keep old people from falling down, as they often do because of muscle weakaness Weight-lifting can benefit women fifty-five to sixty-five years of age, 40 percent of whom, it has been suggested, cannot lift ten pounds, a limitation that severely hampers their daily activities. Still older people, seventy to ninety years old, may benefit even more from a weight-lifting program, and the Tufts researchers have been testing them, too.[5]

Another myth about aging that needs to be dispelled is that as we grow old, we lose our intellectual strength — that ability to learn and to understand, to deal with new, sometimes difficult, situations. Certainly, as we have seen, aging can produce some troubling mental changes that affect judgment and memory. Also, older people have difficulty with what has been called *fluid* thinking — the kind that deals with learning new things quickly and with making complicated decisions. (The elderly seem to have no trouble with what is known as *crystallized* thinking — the kind that deals with vocabulary and depends on all the other bits of knowledge that a person stores up after years of experience.) When people grow old, they often do not have to do many of the mentally demanding things that they had to do when they were younger. They don't have bosses giving them complicated assignments anymore, for example, nor do they have to direct their children's lives any longer. Without such stimulating demands, the elderly can, indeed, "lose it" because they don't "use it."

But aging does not have to mean mental deterioration, and by and large it now appears that some of the losses in memory and intelligence that we hear about in the elderly may be exaggerations. In fact, as long as an old person is physically and mentally healthy, and lives in a stimulating, challenging environment, there seems to be no reason why he or she cannot continue to learn, to grow intellectually. People can even develop their fluid thinking, that is, they can learn new things so long as they are properly motivated and are given extra time to learn. Although it is important that learning be started when a person is young so that a career can get on track before too many years pass, there is no reason why learning has to end when someone is past "college age." Everyone learns at a different rate, and interests shift. A person who hated math during his or her youth may decide later on in life that it would be challenging to pick it up now. It may take a bit longer for an older person to learn, say calculus, but it is certainly not impossible. Old age does not necessarily "put more wrinkles in our minds than on our faces," as the French essayist Michel de Montaigne declared. Indeed, continuing education programs for the elderly are offered just about everywhere — at universities, in local high schools, and through Councils on Aging.

You might ask how elderly individuals can continue to learn if, as we've said, their brains have lost thousands of brain cells — 50,000 to 100,000 every day, to be more precise — none of which are replaced. For a long time, some scientists believed that this steady cell loss, along with age-related deterioration of brain cells, was devastating, that it had to be accompanied by losses in intelligence, or inevitably had to cause senility. It turns out that this bleak forecast may not be accurate. The reason is that we are born with millions more nerve cells than we will ever need, given the limited length of the human life span. Thus, your grandparents and all old persons still have enough cells in their brains for some very efficient thinking, even though the rate of cell death is high. Not only that, but only certain types of the many varieties of brain cells die; when they do, others just naturally take over their function. It appears that only when some disease strikes specifically at the electrochemical functions of the brain cells do we wind up with "aged" minds. "The belief that if you live long enough you will become senile is just wrong," says aging specialist Dr. Robert Butler. "Senility is a sign of disease, not part of the normal aging process."[6] There is. widespread agreement with that. "What can happen is that an older person who is admitted to a hospital for something like a broken hip or heart attack can become confused as a side effect of drugs or simply from the strangeness of the hospital routine," says Dr. Jerry Avorn of the Division on Aging at Harvard Medical School. "The condition is reversible, but the family, or even the physician, doesn't recognize that fact. They assume this is the beginning of senile dementia, and pack the person off to a nursing home. No one knows what exact proportion of people in nursing homes needn't be there, but we have ample clinical evidence that the numbers are large."[7]

The elderly can also learn to improve — or at least coax — their memories by keeping reference books nearby, for example, and by using tricks like hanging an umbrella right outside the door the minute they hear a forecast of rain; if they forget the forecast and head out the door, the umbrella reminds them that bad weather is on its way. They can remember what it was they were planning to say by using simple sentences and refraining from inserting sidelights into any stories they are telling. They can learn to memorize a shopping list by thinking of pictures of items on the list. The psychologist B. F. Skinner has suggested a number of such tricks to help an elderly person's memory. "In the middle of the night," he says, for example, "it occurs to you that you can clarify a passage in the paper you are writing by making a certain change. At your desk the next day you forget to make the change. Again, the solution is to make the change when is occurs to you, using, say, a notepad or a tape recorder kept beside your bed. The problem in old age is not so much how to have ideas as to have them when you can use them. A written or dictated record, consulted from time to time, has the same effect as the umbrella hung on the doorknob. A pocket notebook or recorder helps maximize one's intellectual output by recording one's behavior when it occurs. The practice is helpful at any age but particularly so for the aging scholar. In place of memories, memoranda."[8]

In a sense, learning to improve one's memory, and just learning, are like keeping in good physical shape exercising. Just as they can flex their muscles to keep fit, older people can, in effect, flex their brains to stay sharp. The mind, like the body, can be trained to age well.

The last great myth about the elderly that has to be wiped away is that sexual activity is of no interest to them, or impossible even if there were interest. It may come as a bit of a shock to young people, but sex is not reserved for youth. It does not die with age. Indeed, many of the elderly are not only interested in sex, but perfectly capable of engaging in its many forms. A lot of old people do give up sex for a number of reasons, one of which is the lack of partners. But for countless others, sexual activity is not all that different from what it was when they were younger. It may be less frequent than it was during someone's youth, and there may be some physiological changes in sexual responses that come on with age, but sex is no less exciting or pleasurable than it was during youth.

The biggest difficulty with sex the elderly face is not that they cannot engage in it, but that many young people — especially the sons and daughters of an elderly couple or of an elderly widow or widower — cannot accept an older person's sexuality. This is sad, because a healthy relationship between the sexes, young and old, contributes enormously to one's quality of life. Some scientists have even suggested that a happy marriage and a prolonged active sexual life improve longevity. So, rather than make light of an older person's interest in sex and saying things like "Oh, they're too old for that" or "He's a dirty old man," try to understand that when you disapprove you are reinforcing the negative attitudes toward the elderly that are so common in our society. Moreover, misguided advice will only place more restraints on them, and harm them far more than help them. The elderly have enough restraints on them already, and denying their sexuality can only make them feel that they have fallen, truly, into the ranks of the useless. This observation from Dr. Robert Butler needs to be heeded by all, young and old: "At the very end of life, there is the bittersweet sense that every moment is precious, and sometimes the sense that each encounter may be the last. This is most often poignantly felt by older couples who have met and married very late in life. Those who maintain that the sexual salt loses its savor may be expressing the great difficulty inherent in creating, imaginatively and significantly, the second language of sex. It is difficult to master, but it is a beautiful and satisfying aspect of relating that goes far beyond pure biology."[9]

THE BRIGHT SIDE OF AGE

It is very easy to come away with a negative idea of what aging is all about. All one has to do is look at television advertisements. In many of them, the elderly are applying various preparations for the pains of arthritis, praising some laxative, or smiling broadly to show off new dentures. Young people, on the other hand, are driving sleek cars, wearing fashionable clothes, toning up already flawless bodies in health clubs, or applying beautifying cosmetics to faces that hardly need any help at all.

These images are, of course, stereotypes. As we have seen, not all old people are ill and despairing. Many senior citizens are happy and productive members of society, and the number of such active elderly people is growing. Seniors still preside over nations throughout the world, sit on the U.S. Supreme Court, run major corporations, are stars of stage and screen, paint and sculpt and write books, even run in marathons and climb mountains. The elderly are returning increasingly to school for degrees or just for fun. They are speaking out on issues that affect them through activist organizations like the Gray Panthers; they participate in "Silverhaired

Legislatures," organizations that, though without law-making powers, elect their members from among the elderly and send them to influence bona fide lawmakers in various state legislatures. As Walt Stack, a marathoner in his seventies, once put it, "I may be slowing down a bit, but the important thing is that I'm still out there." And who could argue that President George Bush, at sixty-four the fourth oldest man ever inaugurated, is not a perfect example of an "old" person leading a most productive life? "He is ten years younger than his stated age," his physician once said, alluding to the fact that the President doesn't look his years. "Aging is different in all of us and certainly exercise retards it. I've known him for a long time, and I've never seen him look better. He is very active, very energetic — he tires out most of the people around him."[10] Our third President, Thomas Jefferson, was stamped from the same mold. When he left the White House at age sixty-six, his intellectual powers were not only undiminished, but expanded: he studied science and architecture, Greek and mathematics until he died at eighty-three.

Jefferson's legacy is evident in the present generation of elderly. "Not only are millions living on to Jeffersonian years," wrote Timothy M. James, a senior editor of *The Wilson Quarterly*. "In a way that none of their predecessors could have, the present, huge generation of elders is pioneering what amounts to a new phase of life: a stretch of several years of freedom of a kind that even the flower children of the sixties could not have imagined. Freedom from the burdens of a job, of tending a family, even of the need to earn an income. In the process, they are creating a new culture, the world of the senior citizen."[11]

Of course, it is not only elderly presidents and ex-presidents who have changed our perceptions of old age. There are examples everywhere, some of them well-known individuals, others just ordinary people.

A few years ago, I interviewed the eminent scientist Linus Pauling, when he was approaching his eighty-second birthday. Pauling had won the 1954 Nobel Prize for chemistry and, because of his outspoken hatred of war and nuclear weapons, the 1962 Nobel Prize for peace. When I met him, he was still busy at his Linus Pauling Institute of Science and Medicine in Palo Alto, California, still overseeing the work of his staff, still performing the complex statistical analysis of the institute's results. Moreover, the state of his health was remarkable. He claimed he had never even had a cold —something he attributed to the heavy doses of vitamin C he takes. He was six feet tall and 194 pounds — not the stereotypic image of the stooped old man — and was swimming regularly in his pool. His diet, too, was not what one often associates with the elderly: butter, an egg a day, sometimes two a week with bacon, meat, and vegetables only now and then. "I feel it's my duty to my public to eat them occasionally," he huffed.[12]

B. F. Skinner, the psychologist I mentioned earlier, stands as another inspiring example of someone who conditioned himself to contentment in old age. When I met with him a few years ago, he was seventy-nine and still incredibly active. A professor emeritus at Harvard University, he was getting up at precisely 4:40 A.M. every morning. From 5:00 A.M. to 7:00 A.M., he was at his desk in his study at home. After that, five days a week, it was a brisk, two-and-a-half-mile walk to his office at Harvard, where he wrote and read until exactly noon — and then walked back home. During his seventies alone, Skinner published eight books. He made periodic trips to visit his daughters in London and West Virginia, and to scientific conventions. He told me he received several invitations a week to speak. "But," he said facetiously, "I only go when I'm bribed by an honorary degree, or when they twist my arm."[13] In one of his recent books, Skinner spoke of how young people often do look to the future by exercising and eating carefully. But, he says, they are planning only for a physical old age. A different kind of planning is necessary for the enjoyment of it. For Skinner, part of planning — planning that helped him deal comfortably with his own aging — goes like this: "Instead of complaining of the sere, the yellow leaf, you can enjoy the autumn foliage. Instead of learning to bear the taste of bitter fruit, you can squeeze that last sweet drop of juice from the orange."[14]

Not focusing on the negative, keeping active, and keeping an eye on the future — these are the common denominators that surface again and again when one hears comments from elderly people who are leading happy lives.

Eudora Welty, the writer, at seventy-six: " I can still

see, thank God. I see the mail coming, and the laundry, and friends coming. I want to keep on writing as long as I can think."[15]

Ralph W. Hunter, seventy-four, a retired Los Angeles shipping clerk: "My house is paid for. My car is paid for. Both my sons are grown up. I don't need many new clothes. Every time I go out and eat somewhere, I get a senior citizen's discount. This is the happiest period of my life. These are my golden years."[16]

Reuben Nakian, eighty-seven, of Stamford, Connecticut, an artist: "If I have enough energy I can work like lightning. I get in about three or four good hours a day. I come into the studio about nine or ten and leave about five or six. It feels good just to be in there. I'm not suppose to lift heavy things or drink, but I do. My heart's healed, and I still love to work like hell."[17]

William F. Buckley, Jr., the television commentator and editor of the *National Review:* "I would without hesitation reject an offer of a magical serum that would cause me to become, hesto presto, thirty years younger. Because life is meaningless except insofar as it moves on. Heraclitus taught us that we can never stand twice in the same river: The flow of water — the flow of life — requires, in order that there should be any meaning to what happened yesterday, that yesterday be followed by today; today or tomorrow."[18]

9 ▪
WILL WE EVER
CONQUER AGING?

"Do not try to live forever. You will not succeed."
— George Bernard Shaw (1856–1950)

Most of us, I suppose, envy Methuselah, who lived 969 years before he died. Noah, the ark builder, wasn't far behind: he lived to be 950. Or, in the nonhuman world, we have the likes of the bristlecone pine tree to admire: the oldest living thing on earth, this monument to longevity thrives at well over 4,000 years old in California, Arizona, Utah, and Colorado. One of these ancients, in fact, is appropriately named Methuselah. Located in California, it is more than 4,600 years of age. Not so long ago, another one, in Nevada, died at the age of 4,900. Farther down on the age scale, but still faring better than us mere mortals, are some fish who manage to reach 200 and even 300 years; and some tortoises are still swimming strong after 150 years.

We are not Methuselahs or pine trees or fish, but human beings. And as noted earlier, we have a built-in life span — at least for now and the foreseeable future — of somewhere around one hundred and fifteen years. Compared with some other living things, that's not so bad. We could be flies and live for a single day, a flea for thirty, a white rat for four years, or a dog or a cat who would be lucky to make it beyond twenty. An Indian elephant may be the only animal who seems to parallel our longevity, perhaps hitting the high eighties.

Yet, while we humans fare better than most other living creatures, most of us, especially those of us who are not youths any longer, would agree that things could be better. But will we ever slow that clock of aging we talked about? Will the day come when human beings will be as long-lived as the pine trees, or, settling for less, as some of those Russian fish, sturgeons, who reputedly have lived three times longer than humans could ever hope to live?

For centuries, people have thought long and hard about those questions. Some have only dreamed of extending the human life span, others actually tried to accomplish it. The very foundation of many religions, Christianity among them, is indeed based on the resurrection, the day when humankind will rise from the dead, body and soul, to live not only for a few more hundred years, but forever. There is the Icelandic saga of the man who shed his skin every twenty years or so

and transforms its crudity into a pure, noble and indestructible being."[2] If the recipe failed to provide immortality (which it did), reading it today may at least have one positive effect: it will never fail to drive you to a dictionary.

Probably the most well-known alchemist of all time was an odd man with a formidable name: Theophrastus Bombastus von Hohenheim (1493–1541). He was a Swiss who took the name Paracelsus, meaning that he was greater than a famous writer and physician, Celsus. Paracelsus's father was a doctor, which meant that the alchemist had a large medical library in which to study. But beyond that his medical training came from some questionable sources: astrologers, Gypsies, executioners, barbers, and bartenders. Although he was generally regarded by the legitimate medical profession as a worthless quack, Paracelsus nonetheless worked long hours in his cluttered laboratory, looking for the secret of youth and longevity. Eventually, he claimed to have discovered an elixir that would, in effect, gum up the mechanism of the clock of aging. "Take of mineral gold, or of antimony," he wrote,

> very minutely ground, one pound. Of circulated salt, four pounds. Mix them together and let them digest for four months in horse dung. Thence will be produced a water. Let the pure potion be separated from that which is impure. Coagulate this into a stone, which you will calcine with cenifated wine. Separate again and dissolve upon marble. Let this water putrefy for a month, and thence will be

produced a liquid in which are all the signs as in the first entity of gold or of antimony. Whereof, with good reason, we call this the first entity of these things. . . . Let [this] be put into a good wine, in such quantity that it may be tinged therewith. Having done this, it is prepared for this regimen: Some of the wine must be drunk every day, about dawn, until first all of the nails fall off from the fingers, afterwards from the feet, then the hair and teeth, and lastly the skin be dried up and a new skin produced. When all of this is done, that medicament or potion must be discontinued. And again, new nails, hair and fresh teeth are produced, as well as new skin, and all disease of the body and mind pass away."[3]

It may be assumed that Paracelsus, like all the alchemists of the day, tried his own potion. If he did, it had no positive effect: he died at the age of forty-eight, reportedly of injuries suffered in a tavern brawl. On the other hand, one cannot discount the very real possibility that Paracelsus's brew was poisonous, and that was what killed him.

It is difficult to pay much attention to Paracelsus's researches, given their crackbrain approach. However, in all fairness it should be pointed out that although he was a muddler, Paracelsus may have lucked into a few bits of chemistry that today form the basis of solid medical treatment. For one thing, he was among the first to disregard the popular "humors" theory of sickness and its treatment. This was the belief that four bodily substances — blood, black bile, yellow bile, and phlegm — determined one's physical and mental health. Paracelsus, instead, rightly linked physical to chemical processes, and insisted that if a person was to be restored to health, chemical balance must be restored first. He recognized the healing powers locked up inside inorganic and organic materials, and introduced a number of medicines made from mercury, zinc, lead, sulfur, and iron. Today, many medicines made from the same elements that Paracelsus mixed into his formulas are in wide use. Zinc, for example, which he described as "an elementary substance," is vital to growth and may also protect against high blood pressure. Mercury, a key ingredient in an alchemist's bag of medical tricks, is used in antiseptics. Gold, too, whose power was worshipped by the alchemists, has its uses today: a derivative, sodium aurothiomolate, is a treatment for rheumatoid arthritis; another, auric bromide, is used to treat headache and epilepsy. Paracelsus gave us laudanum, what we now call opium, the narcotic from which the widely prescribed painkiller morphine is made. And there is even a drug named for Paracelsus: *specificum purgans Paracelsi,* or potassium sulfate, used as a laxative.

If Paracelsus's experiments and elixirs seemed unorthodox, they were tame compared with the later work of another "rejuvenator," the French neurologist Charles-Edouard Brown-Séquard (1817–1894). He came up with the radical idea that semen contained substances able to strengthen the body, and that injections of it would restore an old man's weakened mental and physical health. Moreover, he revealed, at the age of seventy-two, that he had mixed the blood and semen from the testicles of dogs and guinea pigs with water, then given himself ten shots of the mixture, in his left arm and in his legs. If you can believe what he said, the results were amazing. Soon after he had the first injection, Brown-Séquard reported, he regained all of the strength he had had years before but had lost. He was now able to work long hours in the laboratory, not even bothering to sit down. He started running up and down stairs, much as he used to do when he was younger. When he stopped taking the injections, he weakened and returned to his slower pace.

Today, we know that the methods Brown-Séquard used to extract the hormones contained in the animals' semen and blood were too crude to provide enough to have the effects he described. The general belief is that the injections acted merely as a placebo, an inactive substance that doctors often give patients to make them think they are getting real medicine. It was probably Brown-Séquard's strong belief that the injections were doing him good that did the trick. That is known as a psychogenic effect, a form of cure that originates in the mind. It is the sort of thing that occurs from time to time when a dying patient is able to postpone dying by demonstrating a fierce will to live. Insofar as sex hormones are concerned, while their production does drop off with advancing age — and replacing them can help in treating some male and female sex-related conditions — this does not mean that hormones have a direct bearing on the aging process. They are connected with some of the symptoms of aging, and indeed hormone balances are vital to the fundamental biological events that are behind aging itself, but that a lack of one or an excess of another causes aging has not yet been demonstrated. Aging, as we have seen, has many causes.

Before we go on to discuss some of the modern-day theories about how our life spans might be lengthened, it is important to draw a distinction between actually slowing the aging clock and lengthening our lives through a disease-fighting approach. Many people believe that if we could wipe out all of the diseases and ills that bedevil human beings, we might live a lot longer than we do. Sadly, that is not the case at all. Even if we somehow managed to escape disease, accident, or death on a battlefield or at the hands of a murderer, most of us would be dead by one hundred. Even if scientists cured cancer, or were able wholly to prevent it, we would add only about two years to our life spans. Even it we conquered heart disease along with cancer and every one of the other major killer diseases, all we might gain would be around twenty years or so, total. That means that all we would be doing is living out our *allotted* life spans — the years dictated by our biological clocks — in a healthier state. We would be free of the threat of a *premature* death, and premature death is what disease and accidents cause. We would not, however, be free of death itself. That, in the absence of disease, will still come anyway. Taking out disease to add a whole lot of years to our life span is somewhat like replacing tires on a car to get it to run longer. What is under the hood, the engine that drives the vehicle, is the vital part. New tires will never improve the car's longevity if the engine is not adjusted and made to run smoothly.

Because aging, as we have seen, takes place at the level of the cell, efforts to make humans run longer and more smoothly are concentrated on what goes on there. One exciting bit of research has to do with organic compounds called free radicals. These are chemical waste products created when various things oxidize, that is, when they are combined with oxygen and undergo a change. The change is called oxidation, and it is the free radicals, roaming about erratically, that cause the decay process that accompanies oxidation. There are many examples of oxidation: the rusting of a piece of iron, the burning of coal or gasoline, the stiffening of a rubber tire or hose, the yellowing of an old newspaper, the spoiling of butter. Oxidation is also at work when paint dries and forms a thick skin, when bananas and potatoes darken after exposure to the air, when the food we eat is burned for energy inside our bodies.

There are clues in all of these reactions for the scientists who are trying to slow the clock of aging. Many of them believe, in fact, that there is little difference between the free radical changes that occur in industrial and natural products and the degenerative changes that occur in our bodies when we age. The free radical theory of aging holds that free radical reactions are what toughen and dry our skin as we grow old just as they dry and crack tires and leather as they age. Free radicals may also weaken or paralyze our immune systems so that we cannot withstand disease. They may even gum up our cells, and mix up the genetic codes that they carry.

If they do all of this — and there is ample evidence that they do — free radicals may well be another kind of biological clock, one that regulates the speed at which we age by regulating the rate at which our bodies oxidize. In turn, then, this means the clock can be tinkered with. If, for example, someone could find a way to stop free radicals from forming, it might mean that the bodily changes that occur with aging could be blocked. Indeed, we know that substances that stop the formation of free radicals, and in so doing have a beneficial effect, exist both in nature and in our bodies. These inhibiting substances are called antioxidants. They are really chemical scavengers because they mop up free radicals whenever the need arises. For instance, some fruit juices, including orange and pineapple juices, contain antioxidants. All one has to do is dip a piece of a freshly cut fruit, like a banana slice, in the juice, and the browning that comes with oxidation will be postponed.

While we have these chemical scavengers in our bodies, there apparently are not enough of them to prevent the buildup over time of damaging free radicals. As we age, in fact, the amount of antioxidants appears to decline. Still, the amount we do have is important. For instance, human beings make more of one antioxidant than does a relative of ours, the chimpanzee, and we live twice as long as chimps.

Because antioxidants seem to have such beneficial

effects, scientists have been looking for some way to add them to the diets of older persons in order to fight off the free radicals that seem to build up with age, and maybe even enable the elderly to live longer. Perhaps the most familiar antioxidant is vitamin E, something you can find on the shelf of your pharmacy or health food store. Vitamin E is found naturally in whole grains and vegetable oils and, as many vitamins do, has a fairly dedicated following among health cultists. Many people consume large quantities of the vitamin in the hope that it will give them youthful skin, improve their sexual performance, and ward off heart attacks and cancer, a few of the diseases it reputedly protects against.

While vitamin E has probably been oversold, like all alleged quick fixes and cure-alls, it nonetheless shows a good deal of promise in the quest for better health, and perhaps longer life, for the elderly. Because it is an effective antioxidant, it does protect cells and tissues from the gradual deterioration caused by oxidation. And, since it is theorized that the effects of aging on the immune system — the body's way of defending itself against disease — are oxidative effects, vitamin E might be used to bolster immunity.[4] One recent study, at the U.S. Department of Agriculture Human Nutrition Research Center on Aging at Tufts University, seems to indicate that such is the case. Researchers gave half of a group of thirty-two people, all over age sixty, vitamin E for thirty days. The other half got a placebo, a pill that had no effect. Neither subjects nor the researchers knew who was getting the real vitamin. Later, tests showed that the people who took the vitamin E had a marked improvement in immune response, including higher levels of the white blood cells that fight off disease. The results of the study confirmed earlier research in which old mice who were fed diets containing ten to fifteen times the recommended allowances of vitamin E developed immune systems that were about the same as those of younger mice.[5]

Other studies with mice and vitamin E had an even more dramatic result. In one, mice who were fed the vitamin not only had stronger immune systems when they aged, but lived longer than other mice. Whether adding vitamin E to a human's diet will have the same effect is not yet known. Testing the effect of any anti-aging additive in humans takes many years. Because of this, researchers have used human cells in test tubes. Some years ago, California scientists added vitamin E to human lung cells, and the cells kept on dividing well beyond the usual life span of such cells. But, unfortunately, when the scientists repeated their experiment many times over, they were unable to duplicate the results of the first one.

Another popular antioxidant is one you've probably eaten if you like cereals. Known in chemical shorthand as BHT, it is added to breakfast cereals or processed foods, like cake mixes, to preserve freshness. Without BHT, or another antioxidant, BHA, packaged foods would survive on the supermarket shelves for only four months or so; with it, the shelf life is extended to a year. Would feeding BHT to a human improve his or her "shelf life"? If just eating cereal did that, we'd all be a lot longer-lived than we are, given the fact that BHA has been added to foods since 1940. There obviously isn't enough of the stuff in our breakfast foods to make a difference, and consuming large quantities of these additives is not recommended. But when scientists cannot test certain substances in humans, they turn, of course, to animals. Some years ago, an eminent researcher in aging, Dr. Denham Harman of the University of Nebraska School of Medicine, tried BHT and other antioxidants on some mice. Mice who were prone to develop cancer were used in his study because they do not live as long as healthy mice. Harman's idea was that if the additives worked, the effect would be more obvious in generally short-lived mice. So, Dr. Harman fed some of the mice BHT or another antioxidant every day; others were not given the antioxidants. The result: the mice who were fed the antioxidants lived longer than the animals who were not, sometimes as much as 25 to 50 percent. Unfortunately, the exact mechanism by which the antioxidants appear to improve longevity is not known. They could, for example, block the cancers that usually affected the mice, or, they could prevent the formation of the free radicals we mentioned earlier. Nonetheless, because of his results, Dr. Harman suggested that if antioxidants were added to a proper diet a person's average age at death might be increased by 10 percent or more. We should add here, however, that not everyone agrees that antioxidants added to one's diet will extend the human life span. Several studies have found no relationship whatsoever between the amount of vitamins taken (vitamins A and C are also under investigation as anti-aging antioxidants) and longevity. While critics agree that age pigments are, indeed, a form of cellular garbage, and that antioxidants may prevent their formation, the general feeling is that the buildup of pigments is not a critical factor in the life span, at least in the mice that have been studied.[6]

Nevertheless, a few other drugs that might prevent age pigments from accumulating are also under investigation. One of these has the imposing name of centrophenoxine. It has an interesting history. Back in the 1950s, a French botanist reported that he threw a batch of it out of his laboratory window after a frustrating incident occurred during an experiment. The chemical fell on a dying, yellow plant and, lo and behold, the plant turned a healthy green. Other researchers became intrigued with the chemical, and started giving it to aged mice and guinea pigs. The animals accumulated less age pigment in their brains and nerve cells and became more active and alert. Not only that, but some of the mice lived longer than expected. One group of mice, in fact, survived for three years — the equivalent of about one hundred years in humans. Fruit flies, too, had their lives extended, sometimes by as much as 30 percent, by the drug.[7] Interestingly, the animals (and some humans who have been given the drug, but with no evidence that they were living longer because of it) lost weight. This has led some scientists to speculate that the drug's possible life-extending effects may somehow be related to weight loss.

That leads us to another approach aimed at slowing the aging clock. It relies not on adding something to one's diet but on cutting something out — notably calories. Calories are, as just about everyone knows, those units of energy that we get from food. Too many can make us fat, too few and we lose weight. We also know that obesity can shorten our lives, and that losing weight often improves our health. But there is also some strong evidence that reducing calories can dramatically extend the life span of mice, rats, chickens, and those very short-lived flies. This may be because fewer calories improves the immune system and lowers the blood levels of dangerous fats, enabling the animals to ward off disease better. Back in the 1930s, Dr. Clive McCay of Cornell performed some classic experiments in which he fed animals a diet that was very low in calories. In one test, rats that had been underfed lived for nearly 1,500 days, while those who ate a normal diet lived only 965 days. It also took longer for diseases to develop in the underfed rats. (To prevent malnutrition, all the animals were given vitamin and mineral supplements.) Over the years, other researchers have repeated the experiments with the same results. The evidence is not so firm in humans, however. Some studies have shown that people whose weight is below average live the longest, but others have come up with the opposite finding that the highest death rates occur among the lowest weight groups.

One scientist who has been studying the life-extending possibilities of low-calorie diets is Dr. Roy Walford of the Medical School of the University of California at Los Angeles. Walford has doubled the life spans of mice by giving them low-calorie diets, and he believes also that there is a high probability of a link between human longevity and caloric reduction, provided the diet includes essential nutrients. "This link has been shown in numerous experiments over forty to fifty years of investigation," he says. "In every species studied — including rodents, and simpler organisms such as insects, fish and worms — restriction of caloric intake markedly retarded aging and extended both life expectancy at any age and maximum potential life span. Inferences from those investigations and at least two direct studies suggest the same will hold for humans. A very gradual weight loss during a period of four to six years, with a high-quality, nutrient-dense diet, might greatly extend the period of youth and middle age, drastically reduce disease incidence and yield a maximum potential life span much greater than the current one."[8] That could mean that our life span could peak at around 140 years instead of the current 115.

While Dr. Walford and others admit that absolute proof of all of this is still lacking, there are some examples among human populations that warrant mentioning. Natives of the Japanese island of Okinawa, for instance, eat a very restricted diet of fish and vegetables, consuming far less calories than Japanese on the mainland. The Okinawans reportedly have a 60 percent lower death rate than other Japanese — and they live to be 100 years old or more at a rate that is up to forty times higher than elsewhere in Japan.[9]

Another group that may have benefited from a low-calorie diet are the superaged people we mentioned earlier, the Abkhasians of the Soviet Union. While some scientists who have visited them insist that the diets of these long-living people are not all that unusual, others say the diets are high in vitamins from the large quantities of fresh vegetables and fruits that are consumed, and far lower in calories than the diet generally eaten in other parts of the Soviet Union. That, along with a hilly environment and a thinner atmosphere that requires considerable physical exertion, may explain the long lives that seem to be so common in the region.

We should point out, however, that not everyone accepts the claims of superage in Abkhazia. Critics have noted that many of the Abkhasians have overstated their age. One reason for this may be that so much respect is given to the elderly. Thus, telling people that one is older than one really is is a sure way for an Abkhasian to gain attention and honor. Another reason may be that men during World War I and World War II falsified their birthdates or used their fathers', thus exaggerating their ages to avoid military service. Later, old people in the region were freed of having to pay heavy taxes on their land and houses, another reason for people to insist that they were older. But things are changing now in Abkhazia. As the older generations die, the next generations find it far more difficult to alter their ages because the government requires proper documentation, a factor that is certain to cause a rapid decline in the number of supercentenarians in the Caucasus. As Soviet critic and age researcher Dr. Zhores Medvedev has put it: "Old traditions are better preserved in the Caucasus than in many other parts of the world. Most people are hospitable and cheerful. Life is probably more enjoyable now in the Caucasus than it is in many other parts of the world. There are new local conditions for a good and long life here, but they do not create miracles."[10]

Reversing the process of aging is, admittedly, an attempt to create a miracle. The barrier is, of course, the fact that aging is caused by so many events that occur in cells, molecules, and body organs. The real miracle would come if scientists ever succeed in intervening in the aging process by manipulating our cells with the technique known as genetic engineering. We are already able to transplant bits of genetic material from one source to another, or fuse different genes together, to create something new, something better. The knowledge exists of the way to give healthy genes to a sick person to cure disease, or transfer genes from a hardy plant to a weaker one to get it to produce more fruits or vegetables. We can give people transfusions of white blood cells to strengthen their immune systems. Would it not be wonderful if we were able to combine some of our genes with those of the long-living bristlecone pine tree and transform our clocks of aging into great-great-grandfather clocks?

Genetic manipulation to directly extend the human life span — that is, not by improving one's health but by interfering with the age process itself — hinges, of course, on whether or not there are such things as aging genes or death genes, or whether errors in the genetic code or accumulated cellular damage are behind the aging process. If these are shown to be more than theories, then it may be possible one day to replace or repair the genes responsible for making us grow old.

It is well to remember, though, that the scientists who are working in aging research are not modern-day Paracelsuses. They are more interested in learning what role cells and whole organ systems have in causing us to age than in seeking a chemical Fountain of Youth. If something that may improve, if not lengthen, our lives emerges from this research, this would be a great plus, of course. But for the moment, scientists are trying to learn more about how to prevent, treat, and postpone the diseases and disorders that can make life so miserable for the elderly. As we said before, wiping out all the diseases that plague us will not allow us to live beyond our seemingly programmed life span, but it most certainly will improve our quality of life. Merely extending the life span without paying attention to disease would create only a huge society of long-lived sick people, many of whom would be disabled and dependent on someone for help.

As matters now stand, science does not know enough to enable us to find the secret of immortality. It also appears highly unlikely that researchers will come up with a single treatment — be it a potion, a hormone, or a vitamin — that will halt or slow down the clock of aging. Aging, again, is too complex a process for any one agent to deal with. For now, it may be best to heed the advice of Satchel Paige, a major league baseball player until he was quite elderly. He listed these six rules for long life: "Avoid fried meats which angry up the blood. If your stomach disputes you, lie down and pacify it with cool thoughts. Keep the juices flowing by jangling around gently as you move. Go very light on the vices such as carrying on in society; the social ramble ain't restful. Avoid running at all times. Don't look back. Something might be gaining on you."

10 ▪

WHAT KIND OF OLD PERSON WILL YOU BE?

"I'm growing fonder of my staff;
  I'm growing dimmer in the eyes;
I'm growing fainter in my laugh;
  I'm growing deeper in my sighs;
I'm growing careless of my dress;
  I'm growing frugal of my gold;
I'm growing wise: I'm growing —
  Yes, I'm growing old!"
—John Godfrey Saxe (1816–1887)

When one is young, time seems to stand still. Old is a long way away, and getting to it is something that happens to your parents and grandparents, not to you. But as we said at the beginning, you started aging from the moment you were born. Your biological clock was wound then and it is ticking now.

Still, it is difficult for you to say for certain just what kind of old person you will be, or what kind or old person you *want* to be. Will you be the same person at sixty-five that you are now? Will you hold the same views? Will you still dance and sing, work and play? Perhaps some of what you have read here will help you answer these questions. Here's what some students your age replied when we asked them what old age had in store for them:

"I believe I will be an active, outgoing person."

"When I am old, I want to be relaxed and rich, and be able to look back on life and be glad that I did what I did and not wish I did anything different."

"As much as I hope that I never get old, I still hope that in later years I am still active and live life to its fullest."

"I want to be an old person who is sorta clued in to the times."

"I hope I will be an old person who can still enjoy my grandchildren's youth and remember what it was to be young."

"I don't think I could stand sitting around all day complaining in pain."

"I want to be independent and self-sufficient. I want to hang out at the barber shop and play the piano at the nursing home. I want to drive a sports car and smoke a pipe."

"I hope to be like a kid when I'm old."

"I hope I will stay young forever, but when I am eighty I would want to change with the society around me."

"I don't like to think about the future or what will happen to me."

"I think I will be just like all the other old people around me, but I will try to stay in good spirits and try to make the most of my old years."

"I would be an old person who will think of the kids today and understand them and the things they do."

"I want to always have the mind of a young person."

"When I get old I think I'll be more active than the average elderly person."

"I'll probably be like any other old person, becoming slower, senile, and not able to hear well."

"I will never grow old."

"I think I'll be the kind of old lady who cares about people and my family and be able to bring my grandchildren where they want to go and be able to do things with them the way my grandmother always does with me."

"I think I'll be all-knowing, wise, advice-giving, wonderful, rich, and in shape."

"I will be very constructive, and always doing something, and never sitting down doing nothing."

"I will be young, maybe just at heart, but I will be young. I don't want to look old."

"I know that I really won't change."

"I am going to be a stingy miser."

"I am not going to crumble into nothing in a nursing home."

"I don't really want to be old, but because I have to, I think I'll be kind of like a guy feeding pigeons in the park."

"I'm going to be the best!"

"I will not be like my parents. I will be laid back and try to have the most enjoyment before I die."

"I would be an old person who minds his own business."

"I'm going to try to do as much as I can for myself and not depend on others. And I'll dye my hair."

"I won't be afraid to use the microwave."

"I'll be a fun-loving old fogy."

"I'm going to be awesome, athletic all the way till the end."

"I plan on enjoying my retirement with some beautiful eighteen-year-old girl."

"I think I will be full of life and ready for a party. I want to be the clown of the party, and I want to live in Florida."

"I hope I will not be bitter. I would like to be full of energy, fun to be around, not an old fart who just sits there all the time feeling sorry for myself."

"I will try not to scorn the views of children."

"I will be like George Burns. Hopefully, I will not look like him, but have the girls and no cigars."

"I think I'm going to be a pain in my kids' ass."

"I will be different from the old people today. But I'll probably be viewed in the same way by young people as they view old people today."

"I will try to be loving, kind, and good-natured. But I may not be able to deliver."

"I'm gonna be like Rodney Dangerfield."

These comments should raise a few questions, not only about the students who made them but about the elderly people they know. For instance, do you think that the students who believe that old age means wrinkles, physical and mental weakness, and gray hair are the ones who paint a sad picture of what their own elderly lives will be like? Are the ones who believe that being old doesn't have anything to do with the number of years that have passed the ones with a more accurate impression of what they'll be like when they are old? Do any of the students' observations reflect the attitude and behavior of their elderly parents or grandparents? If so, which ones? Was the student who said she believed she'd be senile and hard of hearing like other old people influenced in a negative way by the elderly people in her life? What about the views of the student who believes he'll be a pain to his kids when he grows up? Do you think the elderly people he knows are pains to him? Does the student who said she hoped she wouldn't be bitter have a bitter grandparent? How do you think your parents or grandparents would have answered our original question, "What kind of old person will you be?" if they were asked it when they were young? Do you think their answers would have been different from the ones you've just read? Finally, which of the comments most agrees with your own view of what you'll be like later on in life?

I hope that this book will make you think a little bit more about aging, what it is and what it is not. I hope, too, that it will help, even in a small way, to change some of the impressions you have had about the old people you know, especially if you are one who has believed that all old people are the same. And perhaps you may even think about a career in geriatrics.

Old age is something that we all will experience. As a young person, you must prepare for it, but not fearfully or with distaste. Let's close here with this piece of good advice from Leonardo da Vinci, who accomplished much in his later years: "In youth acquire that which may requite you for the deprivations of old age; and if you are mindful that old age has wisdom for its food, you will so exert yourself in youth, that your old age will not lack sustenance." Which is just another way of saying: if you plan ahead, your later years do not have to be sad ones.

CHAPTER NOTES

1. Why Should a Teenager Know About Being Old?

1. B. F. Skinner and M. E. Vaughan, *Enjoy Old Age* (New York: W. W. Norton, 1983), p. 20.

2. Who Are the Elderly?

1. Ken Dychtwald and Mark Zitter, *The Role of the Hospital in an Aging Society: A Blueprint for Action* (Age Wave, Inc., 1986), pp. 18, 26.
2. A. Kalache, "Youth and the Elderly," *World Health* (March 1989), p.8.
3. *Problems Facing Elderly Americans Living Alone*, The Commonwealth Fund Commission (1986).
4. Ibid.
5. Dychtwald and Zitter, p. 18.
6. "The President Is Turning 65," Associated Press (June 17, 1989).
7. Dychtwald and Zitter, p. 400.

3. Why Do We Age?

1. "Age and the Family in the Kalahari," *Research/Penn State* (September 1989), p. 6.
2. Gina Maranto, "Aging: Can We Slow the Inevitable?" *Discover* (December 1984), p. 20.

4. Physical Ailments of the Elderly

1. U.S. Department of Health and Human Services, *How to Cope with Arthritis*, NIH Publication #82-1092 (October 1981).
2. "Can a Driver Be Too Old?" *Time* (January 16, 1989), p. 28.
3. J. Elder, "Older Drivers: Just How Safe?" *New York Times* (April 18, 1987), p. C1.
4. Ibid.
5. "101-Year-Old Driver Calls It Quits," *Washington Post* (September 18, 1986), p. D9.
6. R. Tideiksaar and B. Fletcher, "Keeping the Elderly on Their Feet," *Issues in Science and Technology* (Spring 1989), p. 78.
7. "Hip Fractures Increase among the Nation's Elderly," *MGH News* (Massachusetts General Hospital, Boston, September 1987), p. 1.
8. Ibid., p.4.
9. C. Sempos et al., "The Prevalence of High Blood Cholesterol Levels among Adults in the U.S.," *Journal of the American Medical Association* (July 7, 1989), pp. 45–52.
10. "Alzheimer's Found in Brain Years Before Symptoms Apparent," Washington University School of Medicine news release (1989).
11. L.S. Powell and Katie Courtice, *Alzheimer's Disease: A Guide for Families* (Reading, MA: Addison-Wesley, 1983).

5. Problems with Living

1. D. Rodeheaver and Nancy Datan, "The Challenge of Double Jeopardy: Toward a Mental Health Agenda for Aging Women," *American Psychologist* (August 1988), p. 648.
2. Linda Hubbard, "New Hope for Depression," *Modern Maturity* (1984).
3. "Depression: A Common Problem in the Elderly," Vanderbilt University news release (July–August 1987).
4. Ibid.
5. Rodeheaver and Datan, p. 651.
6. John Langone, "A New Assault

on Shock Therapy," *Discover* (January 1983), p. 55.
7. D. A. Tomb, *Growing Old* (New York: Viking, 1984), p. 106.
8. Ibid.
9. Winifred Gallagher, "The Dark Affliction of Mind and Body," *Discover* (May 1986), p. 69.
10. E. C. Gottschalk, Jr., "Ending It All," *Wall Street Journal* (July 30, 1986), p.1.
11. Ibid.
12. Quoted in Martin Tolchin, "When Long Life Is Too Much: Suicide Rises among the Elderly," *New York Times* (July 19, 1989), p. 1.
13. Ibid.
14. Gottschalk, p. 1.
15. "Alcohol and the Elderly," *British Medical Journal* (June 24, 1989), p. 1660.

6. Putting Down the Elderly
1. Kathleen Fury, "The Ages of Woman," *Working Woman* (March 1985), p. 192.
2. Murray Chass, "New Season for John Starts Same Old Way," *New York Times* (April 5, 1989), p. D26.
3. "Age Proves No Barrier for Reuss-Fisk Battery," Associated Press (April 4, 1989).
4. Gordon White, Jr., "Trevino Grabs Lead with a 67 at Masters," *New York Times* (April 7, 1989), p. A21.
5. William Stockton, "Shooter's Age Is Hot Target of Discussion," *New York Times* (September 12, 1988), p. C14.
6. "Workers Tell State Panel of Age Bias," *New York Times* (November 22, 1985), p. 24.
7. Ibid.

8. Karen DeCrow, "The Significance of Becoming 50," *New York Times* (January 7, 1988), p. A27.
9. "The Future of Older Workers in America: A Work in America Policy Study," Work in America Institute, Inc. (1980), p. 64.
10. "The Sadness of Aging," *Asahi Shimbun*, Tokyo (August 9, 1981), p. 6.
11. Naohiro Yashiro, "Perspectives on the Aging Society," *Japan's Rapidly Growing Population* (Foreign Press Center of Japan, 1982), p. 15.
12. "California Must Address Long-Term Care Needs of Elderly," University of California at San Francisco news release (June 7, 1989).
13. "Generalizations about Older People Are Meaningless," American Medical Association news release (June 5, 1981).

7. How Other Cultures View Old Age
1. David P. Barash, *Aging: An Exploration* (Seattle: University of Washington Press, 1983), pp. 161–163.
2. "Chinese Ways to Help the Old," *Beijing Review* (August 22–28, 1988), p. 39.
3. John Langone, *Long Life* (Boston: Little, Brown, 1978), p. 245.
4. Ibid.
5. Simone de Beauvoir, *The Coming of Age* (New York: G. P. Putnam's Sons, 1972), pp. 75–76.

8. Dispelling Some Myths of Aging
1. Reginald Thomas, "Claude Pepper, Fiery Fighter for Elderly Rights, Dies at 88," *New York Times* (May 31, 1989), p.1.
2. Avis Berman, "When Artists Grow Old," *Art News* (1984).

3. Ellen Brandt, "To Cherish Life," *Parade* (October 16, 1988), p. 4.

4. "Exercise Slows Aging," Federation of Associated Societies of Experimental Biology news release (August–September 1988) and *Journal of Applied Physiology* (August 1988).

5. "You're Never Too Old to Pump Iron," *Tufts University Health Sciences News* (Spring 1988), p. 1.

6. Daniel Goleman, "The Aging Mind Proves Capable of Lifelong Growth," *New York Times* (February 21, 1984), p. C5.

7. Ibid.

8. B. F. Skinner, "Intellectual Self-Management in Old Age," *American Psychologist* (March 1983), p. 240.

9. John Langone, *Long Life* (Boston: Little Brown, 1978), p. 252.

10. "The President Is Turning 65," Associated Press (June 17, 1989).

11. T. M. James, "The Elderly in America," *The Wilson Quarterly* (January 1985), p. 15.

12. John Langone, "Vim, Vigor and Vitamins," *Discover* (November 1982), p. 54.

13. John Langone, "Beyond Reward and Punishment," *Discover* (September 1983), p. 40.

14. B. F. Skinner and M. E. Vaughan, *Enjoy Old Age* (New York: W. W. Norton, 1983), p. 24.

15. Nan Robertson, "Artists in Old Age," *New York Times* (January 22, 1986), p. C1.

16. E. C. Gottschalk, Jr., "Golden Years for Ex-Clerk," *Wall Street Journal* (February 17, 1988), p. 1.

17. Berman, p. 3.

18. W. F. Buckley, Jr., "Reflections on Growing Older," *Modern Maturity* (January 1984).

9. Will We Ever Conquer Aging?

1. John Langone, *Long Life* (Boston: Little, Brown, 1978), p. 16.

2. Ibid., p. 20.

3. Ibid., p. 23.

4. New York Academy of Sciences news release (November 2, 1988).

5. "Vitamin E May Help the Elderly Fight Diseases," Tufts University news release (November 3, 1988).

6. Morton Rothstein, "Biochemical Studies of Aging," *Chemical and Engineering News* (August 11, 1986), p. 35.

7. Langone, pp. 146–147.

8. "Aging Disorders: Will the Challenge Overwhelm the Commitment?" University of Southern California news release (May 29, 1987).

9. Robin Henig, "Can or Should We Conquer Aging?' *Washington Post* (November 24, 1987), p. 36.

10. "Myths about the Caucasian Mountain Centers of Longevity," *Geriatric Medicine Today* (May 1986).

INDEX